MW01529336

THE
CHOCOLATE
PILGRIM

A Journey to Self-discovery & Transformation
On the Camino de Santiago

by

MARIE MACCAGNO

© **Marie Maccagno 2017**

Publisher:
Adventures in Writing
307-2202 Lambert Drive,
Courtenay, British Columbia, Canada V9N 1Z8
maccagno.marie@gmail.com

Cover Design:
Rebecca Frederick of Creative Nobility

Image: Shutterstock _578307079

ISBN 978-1-7750721-0-2 (book)

ISBN 978-1-7750721-1-9 (e-book)

Note to the reader: This book is not intended to dispense psychological or therapeutic advice. The information is provided for educational and inspirational purposes only. In the event, you use any of the information in this book for yourself, which is your constitutional right, the author and publisher assume no responsibility for your actions. In some chapters, names and locations have been changed to protect privacy.

DEDICATION

To all those who support pilgrims on The Way,
the angels and allies who create Camino magic.

ACKNOWLEDGEMENTS

SPECIAL THANKS TO:

Michele Gunderson, coach, guide and friend; Jen Kelly, writing buddy and inner critic-crusher; Love Your Words Mastermind group—all of you, past and present; Cheryl Cohen, editor; Cathleen With, Vancouver Manuscript Intensive mentor; Katherine Marie Tetz, structural editing; Laura Wershler, line and copy editing; Tammy Plunkett and Big Sky Author Services, publishing and business support.

Extra special thanks to my family: Rod, Russell and Emma. I love you beyond measure, and I am so grateful for the times we spend together.

Remember, you don't walk the Camino.
The Camino walks you

ANONYMOUS

THE CHOCOLATE PILGRIM

BEGINNING

RED DEER RIVER

It's the May long weekend and we're on the lower Red Deer River for the third year in a row. Our 18-foot red canoe is loaded with gear for three days of camping. Rod and I have organized the packs to create seats for the kids, and packed everything else to fill empty spaces. I'm paddling on the right, in the bow, Rod in the stern. Russell sits immediately behind me; Emma is seated in front of Rod. Our family loves this section of the Alberta badlands, where we can pull off the river at any point and wander the dry rugged landscape, climbing hills while we search for fossils and remnants of ancient peoples. Rod, with his knowledge of archaeology and geology, contributes his wealth of scientific information during our rambles. When he's around it's like the land is a library revealing its secrets. Rocky outcrops are actually petrified forest remains. That line in the hillside is part of an ancient coral reef. See the white casing on this rock? That means it's a bone fragment from a dinosaur.

I feel like I am paddling back in time as we let the current carry us toward our first campsite. There's an air of magic and anticipation in the air among the four of us, contained within our canoe.

INTRODUCTION

Ten years since the Camino started pulling me in like an ocean tide from over 7000 kilometres away, I'm finally unable to resist any longer. Rod, my husband, Russell, our adult son, and I are packed and ready to fly to Europe tomorrow. It's becoming increasingly clear to me that I'm secretly grappling with difficult feelings about whether I should stay married. I lie awake at night wondering whether Rod and I will ever be able to feel excitement in each other's company again. Yet we're off tomorrow, about to spend six weeks together. Keeping important information quiet is something Rod and I both do well.

From my perspective today, I can see that in choosing to walk the Camino Trail across northern Spain in 2009, I was choosing to travel *toward* something. I grew up among people who regarded violence, abuse, and silence as acceptable, and for most of my life I had been moving away from something both physically and emotionally — from my large and uneven family of origin, from organized religion, from people who make me feel invisible. Ironically, I am seriously thinking about walking away from my marriage at the start of my pilgrimage.

The route we chose, the Camino de Santiago (also known as the Camino Frances) is 780 kilometres long, originating in the Pyrenees in France and crossing northern Spain, ending at the Cathedral located in the city of Santiago de Compostela. Continuing on to the city of Finisterre, on the Atlantic Ocean, adds another eighty kilometres. I originally planned to spend twenty-eight days—four weeks—walking the Camino, having calculated that the entire journey could be completed within that time frame by traveling an average of thirty kilometres a day.

The day I decided to walk the Camino, I was hiking across the Forbidden Plateau in Strathcona Park, Vancouver Island, British Columbia on a twenty-three kilometre-long trail with Rod and three new hiking friends. During the Forbidden Plateau hike one of the women in our party began talking about her bucket list, and the Camino showed up in our conversation. It turned out we all had "walking the Camino" on our lists. As the day progressed, we kept fleshing out the idea of doing the walk together, the time of year we would go, how many days it would take, and how much it would cost; my excitement kept building. By the end of the day I was totally convinced that if I could walk twenty plus kilometres in a day with a pack on my back, I had what it would take to complete such a journey, doing the same thing day after day. I even had a benchmark to make this assessment, since I personally knew someone who wasn't a super-athlete who had walked the trail. By the end of that August day in 2008, feeling high from the walk and strong in my body, I declared I was going to walk the Camino in the spring of 2009.

That day I was fifty-five years old, nearer to fifty-six to be completely honest. I had been an active self-propelled traveller for more than thirty years. However, I wasn't sure how long my body would have the ability to walk long distances. Rod's endurance was more questionable. He'd been diagnosed with Chronic Lymphocytic Leukemia (CLL) in 2005, a slow-to-progress blood cancer. Concern for Rod's health was one of the reasons we decided to move away from Calgary. In 2007 we relocated to Vancouver Island, back to what our son called, "our hippie roots."

Our two young-adult children chose to stay in Calgary. The move seemed sudden to both of them. At the time, our daughter Emma was twenty years old, and living with boyfriend B, a man several years older. As far as I knew, she was spending most of her time playing computer games, MMO's she called them, Massive Multiplayer Online games. She was also an avid reader of fantasy novels. Although she was smart and capable, as a student, she struggled to find reasons to finish her schooling. She had been bullied in junior high, and by high school she withdrew from outside activities, finding it difficult to connect with her peers. As soon as she graduated Grade 12 she moved in with B. She expressed no desire to do any further education. Instead, she wanted a break, and B was encouraging Emma to stay at home rather than look for work.

Our son, Russell, twenty-two, was passionate about playing a trading card game called Magic the Gathering, often described as a combination of chess and bridge. He discovered the game when he was twelve years old and never seemed to tire of the ever-changing elements. He found his niche, working in a store that sold graphic novels and Magic the Gathering cards. Russell's extensive knowledge about the game was an asset to customers since he had been successful in tournament play— winning airfare to play in international competitions in Prague, San Diego, and San Juan in Puerto Rico. He had completed high school in a program for gifted students and earned scholarships to attend university. However, he left the University of Calgary after a year and a half of studying Art History and Music Composition. His rationale? He had no idea about what kind of profession he wanted after graduation, so why spend that kind of money and energy without focus?

Good question. Even so, both Rod and I value higher education, so the choices of our children were challenging to our vision of them moving into adulthood. At times Rod voiced words of disappointment. I, as Mother Bear, would rise to their defence. I kept the lid on my own thoughts. Even though I continued saying the words, "No matter what you choose, I'll support you," I was concerned. *How will they be able to earn a living? Will they always work at minimum wage jobs?* My inner work was accepting that Russell and Emma were making their own way in the world.

In our new home on Vancouver Island, I missed having Emma and Russell living with us. I'd heard about the "empty nest" feeling but I never expected that it would apply to me. Uprooting from Calgary, where I had lived for twenty-eight years, prompted me to re-evaluate everything about my life. What kind of work did I want to do? What groups did I want to join? Who was I now that my children were launched? Did I want to be a wife anymore? How long did Rod have left to live? What will it be like to be left here a widow, when I don't know anyone? The effects of leaving my Calgary network of friends and work colleagues were hitting harder than I ever could have imagined.

I didn't particularly miss moving further away from siblings; I hadn't had the support of an extended family in my life for many years. My parents, Michael and Valentine, had both died several years earlier, my father first in November 2000, followed by my mother in June 2004. Well before my father's death, I made the choice to remove myself from family contact. I surprised my siblings by showing up for both my parents' funerals. Our contact at each gathering was awkward at best.

I've always felt most at ease outside, in forests, beside lakes and rivers, hiking mountain trails. Most of my friendships have been developed through sharing some kind of self-propelled activity—canoeing, hiking, skiing, running. I love doing long day hikes, and have often challenged myself by linking routes together to cover more distance in a day. Prior to spring 2009, the longest continuous hiking journey I had ever done was a seven-day backpack along mountain trails, carrying everything I needed on my back. The notion of walking from one pilgrim refuge to the next for a month without stove, fuel, tent, and all our food for the trip was very appealing.

Pilgrimage felt mysterious to me and I was attracted without understanding what it meant to be a pilgrim. Many who walk one of the Camino routes do so as a Christian pilgrimage because the bones of Saint James (Santiago), one of Christ's apostles, are buried in the crypt at the base of the cathedral in the city of Santiago de Compostela. Pope Alexander III declared Santiago de Compostela a Holy City in 1189. This means that if pilgrims complete a walk during a Holy Year, a year when Saint James' birthday, July 25, falls on a Sunday, they can bypass their time in purgatory altogether. Other years, pilgrims reduce their time in purgatory by half.

Choosing to walk the Camino Frances didn't mean I thought of myself as a traditional pilgrim. I was curious and wanted an adventure. I love to walk. I wasn't prepared to travel alone, so I was grateful that Rod and Russell were also coming along. Although Emma chose not to join us she was with me in spirit throughout my journey.

There were also times when I felt the presence of my mother, Valentine, even though she was safely tucked away in a Calgary cemetery. Had my mother still been alive at the time of planning our Camino, I'm quite certain she would have found some sarcastic words to say about my plan to walk across northern Spain, something that sounded like:

See that short woman, that fat one? My daughter, she's at that stage, you know. That one has always wanted to find herself. Nose in her navel or else in a book. And try to get her to do any work around the house—she'd always disappear and then at the last minute ask if there was anything she could do. Now she says she wants to walk a Camino. She wouldn't even walk a block to the post office to get our mail! She has her head in the clouds, that one. Her and her big ideas. A Camino! Where does she get this stuff from? Find herself. There's nothing to find. But does she ever listen to me? Not that one.

At the same time, I also imagined my mother's unspoken approval of my choice, even if she totally misunderstood my reasons for going on the Camino. Valentine, in her characteristic way of listening yet not listening, always wrapped her own rationale around what I chose to do. She would assume that I was finally returning to my Catholic roots, that I was going to fulfill an important religious duty. Finally I was doing something she could feel excited and proud about in relation to my choice. There were many times I felt Valentine's presence as I planned my journey. Perhaps somewhere on whatever plane she exists on now, she's telling others about her youngest daughter with some pride. *She walked the Camino, that one.*

CHAPTER 1

WHERE I COME FROM

I am born into a family that lives in small town Northern Alberta, "land of the lakes," surrounded by boreal forest. I am the youngest daughter, child number seven in a family of eight. There is a difference of eighteen years between the oldest and youngest, with a split of four older children and four younger. The year I am born, my parents, Valentine and Mike, have been married for twenty years. My father is involved in town politics, currently serving as mayor. He is a man with larger political ambitions, so he often goes out in the evenings to attend meetings, planning sessions, building up his network of potential supporters. My mother is the one responsible for the home front. She's constantly on the move, involved in a number of volunteer activities: Catholic Women's League, working to get Red Cross swimming lessons in our town, School Council, organizing fund-raising efforts for charitable causes.

From the time I am born until the age of seven, we live in a small house on the town's Main Street, railway tracks across the alley behind our backyard. Mom complains about that old house while we are there:

"It's not big enough"

"There's not enough room when we have parties."

"There's only one bathroom."

We still use the outhouse in the backyard where the large garden is, when the indoor bathroom is occupied.

All the bedrooms in that old house are upstairs. Mom and Dad have to walk through the area where four of us sleep to get to their bedroom. My oldest sister, Rita, and I in one bed and middle sister, Annette, and my youngest brother in the other. There are bunk beds downstairs for the rest of the boys, which also serves as playroom and pantry.

Mom and Dad's fights in that house are late at night. When I am awakened by loud voices I sit up, straining to hear what is going on.

"Where were you tonight? I thought your meeting ended at nine."

"I went out with the boys afterwards to play cards."

"I can smell booze on your breath."

"Yeah, we had a few drinks. It was harmless enough."

"What else did you do? Who was there? Were you playing for money?"

"It was the usual crowd. We played poker for small stakes."

"Mike! You told me you wouldn't gamble anymore."

"That's not gambling. Get off my back. I'm tired. Let me get to bed."

"You're hiding something. What else were you up to?"

"Nothing. Now leave me alone."

It is an argument that never really ends. The tension remains during the day even though nothing more is said about another late night.

* * *

I saw Mom work very hard in our old house. We had a wringer washer in the basement, the kind with an agitator within a big tub and two rollers to feed clothes through to squeeze out excess water. After washing, all our laundry had to be hung out on the clothesline to dry. I remember when I was finally old enough to take the clothes off the line and put them into baskets for ironing. I loved the smell of sheets and pillowcases that had been dried outside. I don't remember seeing Dad help with the household chores, at least the ones designated as women's work. He usually came home from work or meetings very tired. He'd give a quick greeting to Mom, maybe a kiss on the cheek, maybe not. Then he'd amble over to the living room, plop down in "his chair," read an article or two in one of the National Geographic magazines piled on the side table, then fall asleep. No matter what we had been doing before dad came home, now we were supposed to tiptoe around him. Mom would shush us, fingers to her lips, "Be quiet. Don't wake up your dad."

We'd do our best to follow mom's orders, but one of the best areas to play with marbles was in our living room where Dad was sleeping. My siblings and I never did figure out how to play quietly, and there was always a point when the noise levels got too high. Waking up Mike was like waking up a bear out of hibernation. Dad would startle out of sleep, roaring, "Stop that noise!" Mom would rush in, clenching her hands with anger. "Didn't I tell you to let your dad sleep?" She'd swat us, clearing my brother and me out of the room, hissing under her breath, "You kids never listen."

Dad didn't have much patience with us younger ones, especially not the girls. He spent most of his time with the older boys, talking about "men's things": politics—local and otherwise—townspeople, possible threats to our family position in the town. After a big meal, my mom and older sisters, along with any available aunts and female cousins cleaned up. I was supposed to help but that wasn't nearly as interesting as other things I could do. Play. Read a book. Eavesdrop on the men in the other room. Woman talk was boring. I didn't want to hear about who just had a baby or who was pregnant. I didn't care about whose marriage was on the rocks. I was always more interested in what the men talked about. So I'd find a place close enough to hear the men and still not be seen by the women, often behind one of the large overstuffed chairs in the living room. Sometimes I would crawl behind the curtains in the room where the men were gathered, making my way ever so slowly to the space where I could hear and still remain hidden. Did they ever see the lump at the bottom of the curtain, or was I invisible?

Mike was the only son in a traditional Italian family that had arrived in Canada from a small village in Italy. Mom was the only daughter from a French-Canadian family. While dad had been raised to expect women to serve him, mom had learned to put men first. In that way, they were a good match. Valentine would jump to please Mike, making sure that he was satisfied with her efforts. If he didn't like whatever she'd done, he was quick to show his displeasure.

"Where's my clean shirt for the meeting tonight?"

"Right here."

"This isn't the one I asked for. How come you didn't iron it? Dammit, woman, why can't you get things right!"

Objects thrown and broken. Mom's tears and crying. Threats. Sometimes hitting.

Dad was more inclined to find fault with things at home, rather than give praise or thanks for all the meals Mom prepared from scratch, like the homemade bread, freshly rolled-out egg noodles for pasta, or the hearty beef stews.

"How come dinner is late?"

"This steak is tough."

"The sauce is too salty."

"Can you shut those kids up?"

Mom's shoulders would slump, her posturing resembling that of a dog expecting to be beaten.

Dad seemed to come and go as he pleased, with little attention paid to the time he said he'd be home. After I left home I learned from one of my siblings that at least once, when my Mom was about to give birth, Dad was supposed to come home at a certain time to give her a ride to the hospital. He didn't show up. One of my older brothers had to go out and borrow a car from a neighbour, getting Valentine to the hospital in time to deliver her baby. By the time I was born, my parents had accumulated twenty years of history, wrapped up in silence and tension. I brought my own energy into the equation. From the time I could walk, I loved running out of our house and wandering out into the streets of our small town, most often with no clothes on. Valentine told me: "The neighbours were always bringing you home, asking if you were my kid."

* * *

Mom has a visitor, one of my older female relatives from the French side of the family, Tante Flora. I have a bunch of relatives like her who all look the same to me: short white hair made whiter with bluing and styled with so much hair spray her hair seems brittle. She's stooped over and wrinkly. Tante Flora smells funny, like she is starting to decay. Her dress is dark and tent-like with sweat stains at the armpits. I'm actually a little afraid of her with that whispery voice all so intense, so I play with my Matchbox toys in the corner of the kitchen while the two women drink tea at the nearby table. My ears are highly tuned to their conversation as I play, because I want to know things.

Tante Flora: "She's getting pretty noisy with those trucks over there."

Mom: "She just can't stay still, that one. Always wants to keep up with the boys."

Tante Flora: "She must be a handful."

Mom: "Too smart for her own good, that one. Give me ten dumb kids over one smart one any day."

*   *   *

Even though Dad doesn't do much to help at home, he works hard to provide for us, spending long hours at his business. Then, in 1955, he is elected as an MLA, a member of the legislative assembly of Alberta, which means he is away even more. However, his increased income allows Dad to custom-build a home nearer to the lakeshore, away from the railroad tracks. When I am eight years old, we move into a house that has more space than I could have believed possible. Three bedrooms upstairs, two bedrooms down, three bathrooms, a large kitchen. Vaulted ceilings in the large living room-dining room area with large mahogany beams. Dad has a den downstairs, his sanctuary away from the noise and demands of his family when he is home.

After we move Valentine talks about how much she misses our old house, as if she loved it the whole time we were there. It is like the way she drives, spending more time looking in the rear-view mirror than she does looking ahead. I love our new house with all its space, room to hide, new furniture and large yard. At the same time I am confused. I want to make sure that I am not too exuberant about the house when mom seems so reluctant to be there. My siblings and I become more distant from each other with the additional room we have, living in our separate worlds.

By this time I've decided that boys have the better deal. I tell myself I'm not a girl. I don't like dolls and I don't enjoy quiet play with other girls. I prefer running around outside, creating imaginary games on the fly with the gang of boys playing in the vacant lot next to our house. My mother does her best to mould me into her image of a presentable girl that she can feel proud of, but I resist her efforts. I like that I am called a tomboy, physically exploring, challenging others, and daring myself to go beyond my own comfort levels.

I feel bored and confined in our home. Performing the typical female chores I am expected to do around the house is not satisfying or exciting to me at all. I am great at pouting and grumbling under my breath when tasked with things I don't want to do. It is a form of resistance. I have already learned not to openly challenge my mother. Punishment is unpredictable, delivered swiftly, like the time I arrive home late for supper because I'd been spending time in Dad's office where he let me play on the adding machine. I walk into the house, feeling great about my time with Dad. There she is, looming over me, holding her "licken" stick. No time for explanation, just the physical beating. I keep hearing the word *liar* as the stick pounds down. When Dad arrives later, he confirms I'd been in his office. I don't remember an apology. By the age of nine I have made a decision for my future self: *When I'm a mom, I'm sure as hell not going to beat my kids.*

In my child-mind I can be or do anything I want. My strongest desire is to become a boy. For several months I concentrate on transformation: *Star light, star bright, first star I see tonight, turn me into a boy.*

I wake up each morning disappointed.

At some point I accept that I cannot change who I am, no matter how much I wish it could be so.

My sense of self is formed around a seed of shame, like the grain of sand around which the pearl grows, shaped by layers of feeling not-lovable, growing up in this family where positive strokes are few and far between. My mother is stingy with her praise. I hear more great things about neighbours and strangers than I ever do about anyone in our family. I hear things like:

"What makes you think you're so smart?"

"Get up off that couch and help in the kitchen right now. Who do you think you are – the Queen of Sheba?"

"Come on, hurry up, we don't have all day. You're so pokey."

"You look dumpy today."

"Don't be such a greedy-guts."

Yet, somehow, my spirit finds the will to carry on in my girl's body. I draw strength from the trees, the lake and the sound of the wind; the smell of dampness and glimpses of spring violets blooming. I'm nurtured by the sound of nothing when I find a secluded spot to sit and take in the beauty of my surroundings. Mother Earth supports me to continue enduring the situation I find myself in.

*   *   *

I started to peel back the hardened layers of my upbringing in 1993—the year I turned forty. Emma was four and Russell had just turned six. Seeing my dad's hand on Emma's elbow triggered a flashback of that same hand on my elbow, and the violation that came next. My whole body reacted as if that moment was still happening, even as Russell and Emma were laughing, and Mom was standing nearby. She seemed to be hovering over Dad as he sat on the floor, ready to swoop in to disrupt his next move. Her posture was protective, aggressive, without any words spoken. Her energy signalled danger, as my body recoiled. I knew I needed some professional help when I found myself flooded with anxiety so profound I couldn't go to work. My three-week leave extended into six months, and finally I left that position to focus on healing.

As my children grew older, memories of my childhood abuse showed up in surprising new ways. Those memories were so painful and so disorienting, I continued with counselling. The more I learned about respectful parenting, the more I learned this wasn't what I had received as a child. I dug beneath the assumptions I had about my family, the biggest one being that we were happy and loving. I began to recognize unhealthy behaviours still present in our family interactions. My commitment to healing ultimately led me to finally step back from family contact, one of the most difficult decisions of my entire life. At the same time, my choice was a profound step toward creating a safe environment for our children.

When Russell and Emma were getting ready to leave home I began to question who I was as a woman and a wife. I reviewed the roles that Rod and I had adopted in our marriage, and wondered if I wanted to keep living in those gender-defined boxes. This was a surprise to me, because the earlier version of me had been so determined to avoid repeating anything that resembled my parents' marriage. Even though Rod contributed a great deal to household chores and was a very involved parent, there were still ways we automatically defaulted to standard cultural prescriptions. Decisions about child care? Marie's department. Decisions about paid work schedules? Rod's arena. Problems with kids at school? Marie's responsibility. Emma needing emotional support? Definitely Mom's time to step up. Given our busy lives and many commitments, role definitions allowed us to function efficiently.

However, I started to feel a lack of emotional connection. I remember thinking: *Efficiency doesn't mean we are still strong as a couple. Even while we amicably divide up the household chores, I'm wondering what Rod is thinking and feeling these days. We hardly ever make time to talk about anything other than the kids, finances, or what has to be done around the house. Does he really want to be with me?*

*   *   *

My questions leave me feeling like I'm treading on dangerous ground, right before I'm about to cover a large amount of ground with him by my side.

CHAPTER 2

DECISIONS AND PREPARATION

In early January 2009, when it comes time to make our travel bookings, the others from our Forbidden Plateau hiking day choose not to commit. Rod and I go ahead with planning. I take time to ask each of our children to join us, having heard inspiring stories of families traveling together. Russell doesn't take long to decide he wants to come; all he has to do is check with his boss about taking the time off. Within ten days, he's finalized his leave from work and how long he plans to be away.

When I ask Emma what she thinks about coming along, she replies, "I'd really like to come but I don't know if I can do it. I'm not very fit right now. All that time on the computer, I hardly leave the house."

She goes on: "You know that there's always two or three days every month where I hardly feel like moving, when I have bad period cramps and just…really heavy flow. Those are days I wouldn't be able to walk. Have you thought about that?"

In truth, I haven't, since I've been period-free for months at a stretch now.

I try using persuasion: "You still have time to get ready. There's at least three months for you to start a walking program. We can have shorter walking days or rest days when you need them."

"Let me think about it," she says.

A week or so later, Emma reveals to me, "I haven't always enjoyed the hiking we did as a family. Those trips were hard for me; I was always at the back. I felt like I was the slowest, the least fit, the weakest link. Everyone else would just push on ahead to get to the top of a mountain pass, and I'd wish I could just sit down or go a lot slower. It's like I was letting you down or disappointing you. This sounds like more of the same."

"I wasn't aware that those times had been so difficult for you. Sure, you let us know you needed to rest, or we had to wait and catch up for you. But we eventually got to our destination."

I admit to her that I did get frustrated at the pace, and what I heard as her complaining.

"Yeah. I hated that. I like to go slow and look around at everything. Sometimes now I don't want to go out walking with you because I know I won't be able to keep up."

This comment cuts into my heart.

"As much as I'd love to go to Europe with you, I just can't imagine doing what you're planning to do. Honestly, I don't think all that walking would be much fun. At least not right now, in the shape I'm in. Especially when I know there are days I know I won't be able to walk at all."

A little later, she reveals more.

"Sometimes I feel so left out, because the three of you seem to enjoy getting out so much. And when you go without me, you come back with all these stories and adventures that I haven't had. It makes me wonder if I fit in with you at all. The stuff I have to talk about doesn't seem very interesting to you, and then I don't know what else to say."

She has a good point. We seem to occupy such different worlds at the moment. I wonder if the love of walking is a genetic thing. If it is, somehow Emma seems to be missing the gene.

"Russell's always been ahead of me. I've never felt like I can measure up. I've stopped trying."

In a flash of recognition, I recall feeling the same way

as a child, believing I could never measure up to Mom's expectations. Never able to keep up with my older brothers. Somehow our family dynamic re-created that experience for my daughter. That was not my intention.

We book flights to Toulouse, France for three: Rod, Russell and myself. We know we can take a train from Toulouse to Biarritz, and transfer to a small train that will take us to Saint Jean Pied de Port, the start of the Camino Frances.

Not knowing how to begin, I get useful information from my friend Nancy, who had walked the Camino with her two adult children in 2004 at the age of fifty-one after completing her master's degree. Nancy told me about how each pilgrim needs to have a *Credencial* before starting on the way. The *Credencial* is a pilgrim passport that allows one to have entry into the inexpensive hostels called *refugios*, or *albergues*, provided for pilgrims along the way. The *Credencial* must be stamped upon every stop at a pilgrim hostel, so the passport then becomes a record of the route a person has travelled. Since pilgrims can only stay one night at each location, the *Credencial* is also a way to ensure that people are moving on, and not taking advantage of the dormitories that are available at low cost for pilgrims. The services are provided to ensure that pilgrimage is accessible to all; finances should not be a barrier. Many *refugios* are *donativo*, which means by donation only. *Albergues* tend to accommodate fewer people and provide a slightly higher level of comfort. One can travel with very little money relatively speaking, depending on choices made for places to stay and eat.

Although we could wait and get our *Credencials* in Saint Jean Pied de Port, I order them in advance from the Canadian Company of Pilgrims, an organization that provides information and support for those interested in walking a Camino. Then I meet a woman named Maybeth who walked the Camino in 2003. She tells me about the Victoria Chapter of the Canadian Company of Pilgrims

6666666

that hosts an annual spring event, with a variety of Camino-related topics and speakers. Maybeth and I drive down to Victoria together in March to attend the day-long Pilgrim Gathering hosted by the group. The timing couldn't have been better.

My questions about what we should take in our backpacks are answered during that Pilgrim Gathering, at a two-hour session offered by a couple who have recently completed their walk. They arrive for their presentation dressed in walking garb, packs loaded, ready for another typical day on the Camino as they proceed to explain the contents of their packs along with reasons for each choice. I make copious notes, and once I arrive home I systematically choose the gear I will take.

At the end of January I commit to at least three training walks each week, doing my best to cover at least ten kilometres each time. When I'm in Courtenay, most often I choose to walk in Seal Bay Park with its Douglas firs, hemlocks and cedars along with the fern and salal undergrowth. I cross-country ski at Mount Washington when I can, another great way to build up my fitness. During the six weeks prior to our departure, I increase distance, and also start walking with my pack on my back, carrying the few items I'm certain I want to take. My sleeping bag, a silk liner, and my old Gore-Tex rain jacket. I'm finding it hard to believe that one can walk the Camino with so little. It's a good thing I attended the Pilgrim Day in Victoria, because otherwise I would have stuffed my pack with heavy non-essentials.

Each week I select more items, place them in my pack and trudge along with that new weight, imagining that I am already on the Camino. As I walk throughout the neighbourhood, people I regularly encounter make comments to me as I go by. The retired woman who is usually weeding in her front yard calls out to me, "You're not making it look fun with that big pack on your back."

A teenager whizzing by on a skateboard remarks, "You

look like you're planning to walk across Canada!"

An elderly gentleman I've never met before stops me to ask, "Are you sure you want to walk with that heavy pack?"

My regular walking companions ask, "Whatever possessed you to decide to walk the Camino? That pack makes it look like you'll be working hard."

Despite the negative commentary, I still feel like I could leap tall buildings in a single bound.

Maybeth loaned books to me that she found useful during her 2003 Camino preparations. I'm reluctant to read much about the Camino in advance. *The Art of Pilgrimage* by Phil Cousineau is one I can't resist. The book is organized according to stages of a pilgrimage with chapters with titles like: "The Longing," "The Call," and "Departure." Cousineau writes about pilgrimage from a historical perspective and also from his own experience. The end of each chapter has specific questions to guide the reader, all related to being a pilgrim. Of course, I don't think of myself a pilgrim but I love books that are introspective, and this one is particularly well written. Although I read the chapters in random order, I find that there is always an invitation for me to ponder more fully what this walk could have in store for me. The idea of "pilgrimage" has long held a sense of mystery, and now I begin to consider the possibility of a deeper opening into life and into yet-unknown aspects of myself.

For much of the time prior to my departure, my work requires that I am based in Calgary preparing a report for a major project. I break up the long hours of technical writing with training walks in Nose Hill Park, one of my favourite locations in Calgary. I replace the coastal rainforests with prairie grassland, hills and coulees, natural paths, and a surprising amount of wildlife for a park within the city.

I like having background music on as I write, so I listen to CKUA, a publicly-funded station based out of

Edmonton. Since I'm an early riser, I often catch episodes of a program called *The Road Home* hosted by Bob Chelmick. The show features an eclectic, heart-felt combination of musical selections and poetry, chosen according to whatever theme or musings Bob might have for that day or week. My listening tastes have softened since I first discovered CKUA over forty years ago. Chelmick has introduced me to poets I've never heard of before and over time, my ears have become tuned to recognize the voices behind those spoken words I've been hearing. It's a little like recognizing a song by the first few notes, or a signature bass riff. I've begun to follow up *The Road Home* episodes by taking books out of the library or going into my local bookstore and browsing for tasty poems. Instead of reading first-hand Camino walking stories and forum posts, I am reading poetry.

I weigh the pros and cons of bringing a book on my walk. Weight is always a factor, but I love reading. I spend time browsing bookshelves in the library, stores, and even my friends' bookshelves. Just before it's time for us to leave, I choose a book of poetry by Billy Collins, *Sailing Alone Around the Room*, a frequent choice on *The Road Home*. I have fallen in love with his poems. Although I am hesitant and not sure why I am doing it, I slip "Billy" into my pack.

Since the fall of 2008 I've been working at a new job with an environmental consulting company based in Calgary. My job title is Traditional Knowledge Facilitator; I create reports based on oral histories recorded from Indigenous people in northern Alberta affected by resource developments on traditional lands. We prepare traditional land use studies from all the interviews we collect, and use the information to prepare reports for different purposes. Sometimes it's directly for a First Nation, sometimes it's for a company that wants to start a major industrial development and the regulatory body that requires environmental assessment. I look forward to going out into communities and holding the interviews; I love the process of getting to know people and listening deeply to the answers I receive to my questions. I get paid well for what I do, and I relish my newfound sense of financial freedom. The work I do gives a new purpose to my life.

I spend enough time in Calgary that Rod and I decide to buy a three-bedroom townhouse as a second home. I move in January 2009, along with Russell and two of his friends as my roommates. I've made it clear to everyone that I am just another roommate; I am not "Mom." I come and go as I need to without feeling responsible for anyone else. My time in Calgary is like a pilot project, where I get to re-create myself away from the roles of mother and wife. My new level of financial independence makes me feel like I have wings. It's at this time that I start writing a blog where I report on my observations from this new way of seeing the world.

I return home to the Comox Valley no longer content to be the same Marie I was prior to our move to Vancouver Island, when my energy had been directed mainly to the well-being of my husband and family. I make new decisions about whether to continue keeping silent regarding Rod's leukemia diagnosis. His original request had been, "Don't tell anyone."

It took him almost three months to tell me his blood test results. And it took another two months of us holding the silence together until I finally insisted, "Our kids need to know. I'd prefer if you tell them, but if you don't, I will. They can tell something's wrong, and they're starting to make up stories about what might be going on. This doesn't feel right to me."

Rod chose to tell them at a time when we were all together on a vacation. We came together in a new way, difficult as it was. Both Russell and Emma were shaken, yet strong in their willingness to hold Rod within our family circle of support.

The silence about leukemia carries on into our new community. He tells me, "I don't want people to look at me with pity in their eyes."

I think, *What about those people who want to love you and support you?* I do my best to avoid telling anyone about the diagnosis. Finally, I have to let Rod know how I'm feeling. I tell him "I can't just pretend that everything is fine, when sometimes knowing you have leukemia is so painful I can hardly stand it. I need to have a couple of friends that I can talk to when I feel this way, because talking really helps me. And I need people apart from our family to open up with."

"Well, if you really need to talk, I'm not going to say you can't. Could you at least let me know who you've shared my diagnosis with?"

"That I can do," I say.

I no longer gloss over the ways I feel dismissed or overlooked. A typical scenario might be when we're going out for an evening. Rod leaves the house first, while I'm still getting my shoes or boots on. He'll have been reading or quietly doing something on the computer, and then all of a sudden, jump up and announce, "Time to go!" He turns off the lights as he goes, leaving me in the dark. Unkind thoughts flood my senses: *Maybe you should go on your own then. What's the big rush all of a sudden?*

I feel like I don't matter; frustrated, brushed off, unimportant. The rest of my evening is coloured by Rod's exit, as I hang on to my sense of injury.

I can easily flare into anger with other patterns in our relationship, like the way Rod deflects suggestions or ideas I want to discuss. He is a master at avoiding answering questions directly.

Me: "Would you be interested in going on a week-long backpack in August?"

Rod: "Yeah, we could go canoeing on the Red Deer River."

Me (self-talk): *What? There's hardly any water in the river then. That's a terrible time to go. How did you jump from backpacking to canoeing?*

Me (out loud): "Is this your way of saying no to backpacking?"

Rod: "Whatever gave you that idea?"

I don't know whether he deliberately communicates this way or not. Does he really want to keep me from knowing what he'd truly prefer? Sometimes he tells me I don't understand his sense of humour, that this is his attempt at being funny. And he's right. I'm not laughing.

As I spend more time working away from the Comox Valley, I'm also wondering: *Where is home?* I feel as if I've got one foot on Vancouver Island and another foot in Calgary. I am not sure whether I will stay in my marriage. At night when I have trouble sleeping, my mind endlessly turns over possibilities: *If I choose to leave Rod, could I make a new life for myself here in Calgary? How do I know if I should leave or stay? Is our apparent calm and contentment just a way of maintaining the status quo? Is it more about staying with what's familiar than going for something much bigger?*

Shouldn't I feel more excitement with my partner? Especially after twenty-five years of marriage! At one point, feeling especially brave, I say to Rod, "Just because we don't fight doesn't mean everything between us is great."

He asks, "What does that mean?"

I don't feel courageous enough to honestly answer his question so I tap dance around what I would love to say. Which is:

There's a lot going on inside right now that I can't talk about. I am feeling a lack of passion between us, like we've settled into a routine where we're both kind of bored with each other. This isn't how I want to live. I'm just starting off on a great adventure, now that I've got this great job and no kids to look after. I don't know if you'd understand how unsettled I am, or how you would respond if I tell you. I imagine that you would sit there waiting for me to sort things out for myself. Would you try to fight for me, find a way to convince me to stay if I said I want to leave?

I don't know if this Camino journey will bring us any closer together or better able to talk to each other. Yet, that is what I hope and dream of.

I have never organized an adventure like this before so it is hard to imagine what it will be like to walk the daily distances, day after day. It's like trying to imagine how much a billion dollars is; all those zeroes are quite meaningless. The 880 kilometres from Saint Jean Pied de Port to Finisterre will be just a heck of a lot of steps. Within my happy little bubble of imagination everything will work out. In my imaginary world I have abilities that spring forth completely formed without any prior training or exposure to the skills required. Thus, I boldly plan our journey with big daily distances in mind. I construct a Marie who is capable of easily walking thirty to thirty-five kilometres a day for the entire pilgrimage route. I blithely added on an extra ten kilometres per day, because I think I'm that strong. I will have no physical hardship, and my relationships will be easy-going and amicable. I'll be calm and serene, and enjoy all the people I meet along the route.

Besides, my pack is still smaller than anything I have ever carried on a multi-day journey.

Rod and I arrive in Calgary a week before our departure in order to spend time in our threesome coordinating gear selection, sharing route information, and planning our travel in Europe before and after we are finished our long walk.

> Me: "I've got these guidebooks if either of you want to read things over and get more details. I'm so busy right now, it's hard for me to focus on our trip."

> Rod: "I can do that. I haven't done much research yet. I've been letting you take the lead on this one."

> Russell: "Yeah, I'm okay with whatever you guys decide. I just want to go walking in Europe."

> Me: "What do you think about planning to walk about thirty kilometres a day, and finding *refugios* to stay at once we're finished for the day? I don't want to have everything planned in advance."

> Rod and Russell: "Good idea. I think that's the best way to go. We'll figure things out when we're on the trail."

There's something else that's been weighing on my mind, that I finally bring up when all three of us are together.

"I'm most interested in walking to Finisterre on the Atlantic Ocean, another eighty kilometres beyond Santiago. I've done some reading, and the more I find out, the more I want Finisterre to be my end point. This is the place where ancient Celts worshiped and built a Temple to the Sun. Even though that temple doesn't exist now, knowing that earlier people journeyed to the ocean along the present-day Camino route appeals to me far more than the Christian ending in Santiago."

Rod wants to know more, and Russell is intrigued, so I elaborate: "Reading I've done about the history of the Camino suggests that the Celts had a version of the route that followed the Milky Way—*via lactea*—which ended at *Finis Terre*—end of the earth. I love the idea of following the stars to the ocean."

Russell speaks up: "I've been describing myself as a spiritual nomad for quite a while. I like this idea. Count me in!"

I'm not surprised, since Russell has not been part of any organized religion since Rod and I left the Catholic faith when Russell was six years old and Emma was four.

I have always felt most connected to spirit when I am outside in nature rather than inside of buildings constructed for worship. Rod's relationship is somewhat more complex. While he's drawn to non-Christian spiritual practices, I've noticed he has an enormous sense of guilt for not following Catholic prescriptions and traditions. It seems to be a constant push-pull in his decision making. I remember a time when we were visiting Rod's dad, Bernie, in Victoria, after we had decided to leave the Catholic Church. I no longer attended any Catholic mass, and I wasn't forcing our kids to go to church either. Bernie was very devout, and expected that his son and family would follow his lead. When I refused to go to church with him and Rod, Bernie was very upset. He never forgave me for my choice. Rod was the only member of our family that continued to go to church with his dad.

Rod: "I'm not so sure, but if you two want to get to Finisterre so much, I'll go along with this plan. Are you sure you want to add on the extra kilometres?"

Me: "Absolutely!"

Russell: "You bet."

So we finalize our travel itinerary from the time we

fly out of Calgary until we arrive in Saint Jean Pied de Port, France on April 18, 2009. We will start walking on April 19. From that point onward we have no fixed itinerary. We will make our way with guidebooks and maps; whatever we need will be on our backs. I trust my feet are ready for all the steps I need to take in order to complete this journey.

CHAPTER 3

APRIL 16, 17, AND 18TH
TOULOUSE AND ARRIVAL AT
ST. JEAN PIED DE PORT, FRANCE

Our two-hour flight from Frankfurt to Toulouse lands in the late afternoon. We plan to spend two nights in Toulouse upon the advice of more seasoned travellers:

> "Give yourselves time to adjust to the new time zone."

> "There's interesting museums and sights to see in Toulouse."

> "Take in some of the French cuisine."

Once we've settled into our accommodation, we set out on a walking quest to find a place to eat our evening meal. What we discover is a nondescript restaurant in a nearby small strip mall that surprises us by what we find inside. As we enter the doorway, we are greeted by an inviting atmosphere. The walls are soft pastel colours, quiet music plays in the background. An attentive host quietly makes his way to our party of three, leading us to a round table covered with a white tablecloth.

Menus are placed carefully in front of each place setting. There are so many mouth-watering options, it's hard to make a choice. Russell appreciates good food, and his attitude is contagious here. Looking for something I'll enjoy that isn't too carb-laden, I finally decide to order poached fish. Russell is more adventurous, choosing food he's never eaten before—beef tartar. Rod looks at menu prices and requests ravioli since the pasta dishes are the least expensive. We also order a bottle of dry white wine to enjoy with our meal. We are in France after all.

The wine is brought out first and expertly poured into our glasses. We lift our glasses to celebrate how far we've travelled in a short time. "We're in France!" I exclaim in wonder. Rod and Russell grin back at me, like we're all children again. Another waiter appears with a plate of warm bread wrapped in a linen cloth, with an accompaniment of soft butter. "I didn't know how hungry I am," I state to the others. "Me too," says Rod. When our main courses arrive, all that's left of the bread is crumbs on the tablecloth. We take in the beautiful presentation and the aroma of well-prepared food. Next we silently take our first bite, followed by eye contact and exclamations.

"Wow, this fish is so well-cooked, and I love the lemon sauce that comes with it."

"Beef tartar is not what I expected, but I like it."

"I wasn't sure how well a French restaurant would make seafood ravioli, but this is great. The creamy sauce goes so well with the filling."

I do my best to monitor my food intake, no matter where I am. Even though I'm getting caught up in this beautiful moment, the French cuisine, and our celebratory state of mind, I can already feel a knot of anxiety in my chest about putting on weight.

"Hey Russell, I can't finish my fish and vegetables. Do you still have room?"

"Really? You can't eat that?"

"Yeah, I'm totally full right now. I probably had too much bread while I waited for the main course to arrive."

Russell gleefully pushes his empty plate over to me, while I slide mine toward him. "How can you eat so much?" I ask. "No wonder we call you the man with a hollow leg." Rod is another man who loves to eat and he doesn't hesitate to clean off his plate.

"Hey Rod, aren't you going to share your ravioli with Russell?"

"No way!" There's no plate-swapping between the two men.

They revel in finishing off their meals as I sip my wine and think I should have resisted that last piece of bread.

Although we have limited access to public transit for getting us into the city core, we manage. It's a good thing we all like walking and have a pilgrim mind-set. Toulouse has some attractive historic buildings and small parks to rest in when we need breaks. "I love this city. I think it's beautiful." Russell replies, "Prague is nicer." I shrug my shoulders. I can't offer any rebuttal to that statement since I've never been there.

We are choosing to explore without having done much research about points of interest. In our wanderings, we stumble upon the Basilica of Saint Sernin. When I enter, I see a sign announcing that this is a pilgrim stop on one of the French routes to Santiago. Under the sign is a table with a rubber stamp and ink pad so we stamp our pilgrim *Credencials* with their very first Camino stamp. "This is it, we've started our Camino!" I exclaim. Rod and Russell try to ignore me, obviously not as excited as I am. As I explore the inside of the basilica, which has separate alcoves for honouring different saints in Catholic theology, I am attracted to the statue of Saint Anthony. I don't feel any connection to the images of Christ on the cross, or the icons of Mary holding her infant. After making a full circuit of the interior, I return to Saint Anthony and light my first candle on this journey. As I strike the match and hold the flame to the candle wick, I offer a loving prayer for Emma. "May you continue to grow and find your way in this confusing world we live in. May you feel this love I send you, and know how much I appreciate who you are." Lighting the candle has a calming effect as I anchor myself in thoughts of well-being for someone I love. I decide to continue this ritual whenever I enter a church.

Our time in Toulouse marks the beginning of making collective decisions, choosing where we want to go and then finding our way. Patterns emerge quickly. I do some research, talk to people, and decide on what might be interesting places for us to visit. Rod and Russell are the navigators, able to figure out maps and schedules very quickly, while I feel quite lost in a sea of information I'm not able to organize in my mind. I am relying heavily on their guidance to get us where we've decided to go.

Russell states his request: "There's an area in Toulouse that sells graphic novels and music CDs. I want to check it out." I know that Russell is passionate about music, but his passion for graphic novels is new territory for me. I'm surprised when he pulls out a sheet of paper with store names and addresses, which he matches up against the city map Rod is holding. After a quick scan, Russell leads us to a street with two stores on his list. Now it's his turn to be excited. "Wow, look at these books! I can't get these in Canada. There are so many great European graphic novelists." Russell lovingly pulls books off the shelves to look at the art work and shows me one of his all-time favourites. "This is Moebius. His work is not readily available in North America. Even though I work at Phoenix, I can't order this one. Look at this detailed art work, it's so precise." He takes time to show me an Enki Bilal graphic novel. "Here's another graphic novelist I can't order into Canada. His books have won so many awards." He reluctantly leaves each store without making a single purchase.

The novelty of being in Europe has us in high spirits during our explorations. Rod and I are treating each other more like friends at this point. We are polite, keeping each other at arm's length, like we're checking each other out. He's probably asking himself, *What will Marie be like on this journey?* I'm wondering, *How are we going to manage for another four weeks?* I'm already noticing that I am quick to react with impatience toward Rod when he doesn't directly state what he wants. Standing outside one museum, he asks, "Do you want to go in here?" I say "No" because I am not that interested. His face registers disappointment. I realize, too late, that he really wanted to go inside. Why didn't he just say, "I'd like to go into this museum. Would you come with me?" I would have said yes. Later, when we're taking a break in a small park, he goes off down the street. I see him returning with ice cream cones for us all. I feel anything but grateful. *He didn't ask if I wanted a cone. I'm not even hungry. Now I'm going to have to eat this ice cream.* I'm frustrated, given my obsession with avoiding eating too much. Both Rod and Russell happily dive in while I reluctantly nibble at mine. I wonder, *Why is it so hard for me to let down my guard about gifts of food?* I offer my half-eaten cone to Rod to finish. I can only hope that walking thirty kilometres a day will free me up from worrying about food intake.

The single bedroom we share with Russell keeps Rod and I at the "we're just friends" level of contact. Rod's never been comfortable with public displays of affection, which has often caused me to feel rejected. Sometimes he avoids the simplest gesture, like holding hands in public, even after being together all these years. Rod is even more restrained in Russell's presence. Given my questions about the state of our relationship, I'm relieved to have this space. I'm not feeling much desire for physical contact or closeness at the moment. Travelling with our son helps me hold my sharp tongue when I'm thinking unkind thoughts. There are moments when I'm painfully aware that I'm still trying to decide how much I like my husband, let alone whether or not I love him.

I do admire Rod's ability to navigate in unfamiliar places. Both he and Russell have figured out the transit schedules so quickly that I have no time to piece the numbers together for myself. When I ask Russell, he gives me a patient explanation that I understand. Rod rolls his eyes as if to say, *How could anyone need an explanation for something so simple?* Even so, this is good information for me to have since I worry that if I am ever separated from these two men, I'd be so lost I wouldn't know where to begin. That is one of my bigger fears, especially in the large cities, being alone where I don't speak the language well, not knowing where I am or how to find my way.

After two and a half days of romping through Toulouse, it is time to catch the train to Biarritz and on to Saint Jean. Working out what train we need to take, what platform to get to, and how to pay for our travel is even more overwhelming than using public transit. Once again, Rod and Russell recognize the patterns. "We have to get to Platform 23. The train leaves in twenty minutes." The crowd presses in on us, and we're all feeling a sense of urgency. I spot what we're looking for, "There, Platform 23!" I point at the sign, which Rod and Russell haven't seen. Relieved to be in the right place, we find a pillar to rest against until the train arrives. I'm feeling over-stimulated by all the noise, the confusing electronic screens, and the volume of human activity all around me. I'm so ready to get onto a quiet trail. I gratefully take a place on the train and sit down.

Breathe.

Look out the window.

Breathe.

Our train ride to Biarritz is uneventful, much to my relief. We disembark, and after a short wait we board a single-car, slow-moving train that takes us from Biarritz to Saint Jean Pied de Port. There are a few passengers who look like pilgrim-types, although I do not make any effort to communicate with any of them. I am already turning inward, full of mixed emotions—excitement, fear, joy, anxiety—as we approach the end of our train travel. Just getting to Saint Jean feels like a pilgrimage within a pilgrimage, this village I have read about and dreamed of for weeks.

First order of the day? Find the building where pilgrims can register for the start of this journey. Saint Jean is very small so it's not hard to find the community hall furnished with one long table and many chairs. Several volunteers sit at the table, with a card in front of each person identifying the languages they speak. I immediately head over to the person with "English" written on a card. As we are being served, other pilgrims enter the room. I recognize some of them from the train ride from Biarritz. Since we already have our pilgrim *Credencials*, our time in the hall is brief. We complete our visit by collecting a stamp and heading out the door. Once we find a *refugio* for the night, we go off exploring Saint Jean. One of our guidebooks suggests visiting the ramparts of a 17th century citadel at the top of the hill overlooking the village. We walk up Rue de la Citadelle, the narrow main street, marvelling that we are here.

I ask the two men, "Do you want to look for a market to buy food for making our supper?"

Rod replies, "I think that will be a lot of extra work. I don't feel like cooking tonight, and I'm not really interested in cooking our own meals while we're walking."

Russell speaks up, "Yeah, I think we should just eat out. Restaurant food won't be that expensive, especially if we choose from the pilgrim menu."

I'm not quite ready to give up. "Many of the *refugios* along the way have communal cooking facilities and eating areas. I don't think making our meals would be that hard. It could end up saving us a lot of money." And although I don't say this out loud, I'm thinking about how preparing our own meals would save me a lot of calories.

Rod is quick to counter. "Can you picture us arriving in a town, tired after a long day, and we still have to decide what we're going to make, then find a store where we can buy the ingredients? That doesn't seem practical. I think we should eat out, starting tonight."

So we make our decision to eat supper meals in restaurants, rather than look for *refugios* with cooking facilities. Originally I intended to prepare all of our supper meals, but I'd never stated that clearly. I've accepted the wisdom in the men's thinking, although I think to myself, *I guess we'll miss out on meeting up with other walkers in shared kitchen space.* Without admitting it to myself, I had been looking forward to that experience.

I honestly can't remember our meal that first night, too excited to pay much attention to the food. What I do recall is exploring the village, wandering up to the top of the hill overlooking the town, feeling awestruck at the scenes that lay before us. Red-roofed houses, green hillsides shrouded in mist and, where visible, flocks of sheep looking like white dots on the landscape. That peaceful view mirrors our idyllic overnight stay as pilgrims in Saint Jean Pied de Port. We are housed in a large old building with a room to ourselves and several beds to choose from. If this is what traveling on the Camino will be like, I gleefully anticipate the thought of what lies ahead. Our *hospitalero*, an older man, tells us he has walked the Camino eight times; he speaks of the Camino with great reverence. *There's obviously something to this pilgrimage thing,* I think to myself.

Just before I fall asleep I open my book to read a poem from Billy Collins. The pages fall open to "The Rival Poet." I especially like the reference to "In my revenge daydream…." My eyes linger on those words.

CHAPTER 4

APRIL 19, DAY 1
SAINT JEAN TO RONCESVALLES, SPAIN
(25.5 KM)

Before I step outside this morning I select one of the eight tiny polished stones I brought with me for offerings. I agonized whether I should bring these small objects, aware I was adding extra weight to my pack. I choose hematite to leave at the base of the statue of Saint Anthony. Yes, he's here, along with an icon of Saint James. My wishes are for grounding and safe travels. Standing outside on the street, I am quite teary-eyed. The *hospitalero* takes our photograph beside the door of our *refugio*, and his parting words are, "Remember. You don't walk the Camino, the Camino walks you."

As we walk through the village of Saint Jean, we decide to get some lunch supplies. While Rod goes off in search of bread from one of the nearby patisseries, Russell and I scout out the shops that carry meat and cheese. When we reunite, Rod is holding two loaves of bread.

"TWO loaves of bread? Where are we going to put those big loaves, in our already big packs?" My voice rises, almost to a shriek.

"I haven't been eating bread for months now. Do you think we're going to eat that much?"

What is this man thinking? I am livid! Full of anger, beginning at the base of my spine and expanding out to my indignant words.

All Rod can do is shake his head in bewilderment as

he replies, "I was just trying to get you something special."

I feel sick to my stomach. It's a moment of agony in the middle of my joy and excitement. I'm curious about my strong reaction and the way my rage flares up so suddenly. Just as quickly as a memory.

*   *   *

It's Christmas time. Our large family comes together every Christmas and the adults are generous with the presents. My father, Mike, has put the largest box of all under the tree. My eight-year old self is curious, so as soon as he's out of the room I crawl over to see who it's for. It's Mom. "To Valentine, from your ever-loving Mike," reads the tag. My curiosity slips to envy; it's not for me. True to family tradition, after Midnight Mass on Christmas Eve, we begin to work through the pile of presents under the tree. Gift opening takes a long time to complete, with each item held up for others to admire.

My oldest brother says, "Oh, what a beautiful hand knit sweater. Thanks, Mom!"

My sisters chorus, "Try it on, let's have a look."

My youngest brother says, "Hey, an Etch-a-Sketch!"

I shift that big box over to Mom. "Here's a big one for you."

Mom sets it to one side. I wonder, *How come she's not opening that present?* More gifts are unwrapped.

I say, "More Lego!"

One of my older brothers says: "This is a great beer stein."

Finally, the big box from Mike is the only present left and Mom can't avoid it any longer. She opens the package, revealing the words Holt Renfrew on the box. Inside is a stunning fur coat. "Oh Mike, you shouldn't have."

"Try it on," Dad urges her.

"I can't. This is too much."

We all insist. "Mom, put it on!!"
Dad holds the coat for Mom as she reluctantly slips
her arms into the sleeves. Dad's gift fits her beautifully,
and I think Mom looks like one of the movie stars in the
magazines she loves to read. Exclamations echo around
the room.
"Mom, you look gorgeous. Dad, how did you know
how perfectly the coat would fit?"
Valentine finally speaks, her jaw held tight, no hint
of a smile. "I can't keep this. We can't afford it." I am
puzzled by the tension in this exchange.
Focus in the room shifts, as my oldest sister comes
into the room. "It's time to eat! Come on everyone, the
table is set." I never see Valentine wear that coat again.
Soon afterward, our kitchen counter has a new toaster
that toasts up to six slices of bread at one time.

*   *   *

Walking brings me back to myself, to where I am on the
High Route over the Pyrenees. Today is one of the first
days this season that this section of the Camino is open
to hikers. The day starts out clear as we leave Saint Jean.
During our gradual ascent we are surrounded by patches
of green pasture pock-marked with sheep. I am grateful
the route is so well-marked. I expected we might have
difficulty navigating, and what we've found so far is that
blue and yellow scallop shell markers appear at every
junction, with yellow arrows indicating the direction to
follow. The higher we climb, the more the mountain
hillsides are obscured by low-lying fog, which creates a
sense of mystery to our surroundings. At the highest
elevation, temperatures drop, snow begins falling, and
we need to stop to add another layer of clothing. Clouds
are so low, all we can see at this point is the trail and the
occasional scallop-shell marker indicating the way.
Now I understand why the High Route is not always

open to pilgrims. Today we are part of a small number brave or foolish enough to hike over the mountain pass.

"This reminds me of mountain trails in Banff National Park."

"I wonder if it will always be this quiet on the Camino. We picked a great time to come."

We stop briefly at a sign that announces, "You are here." We look at each other, laughing. "Are you here?" "Yes, I am." Keep walking, one foot in front of the other, slowly climbing until we arrive at a monument by the trail indicating the distance to Santiago: 765 kms. We stop for photographs, adding layers of clothing to keep warm. My earlier outburst is forgotten as we enjoy our surroundings. My emotions are as up and down as the Pyrenees.

We cautiously make our way off the pass, following the route markers down to Roncesvalles. There's a surprising amount of snow accumulation on this side of the Pyrenees, with packed boot prints guiding us along. We've walked in conditions like this in the Canadian Rockies, so we're quite confident moving through this section. Finally, we drop down enough that we're hiking on a muddy trail, with snow lining the path.

And then my spirits lift. In the distance, we can see the building that will be our home for the night. Twenty-five kilometres of walking and 1300 metres of elevation gain and loss later, we arrive at Roncesvalles in Spain.

I break through my shell of silence with strangers during our supper in Roncesvalles. The *refugio* provides a meal for the pilgrims who choose that option, which we do. Not yet knowing the rules, we arrive a few minutes late to dinner (a no-no in pilgrim-land!)

As a result, Rod, Russell, and I have to split up and sit at different tables. Bowls of soup are in front of each place, so I find an empty chair. Everyone else is already enjoying the hot kale and bean soup, speaking mostly in languages other than English. I feel lost in this large room, sitting with seven people I've never met before, listening to a sea of foreign voices. Finally I work up my courage and hesitantly ask the young man beside me, "Do you speak English?" To my relief, I hear him say, "Yes." He tells me, "My name is Norman, and I am from Cologne in Germany." His companion says, "I'm Sebastian, I am also from Cologne." Sebastian is less fluent in English, but we three are able to make conversation throughout the meal. Norman informs me, "We have walked from Germany. We are juggling and making music in the bigger towns and cities, earning money from our busking. We plan to be away from home for at least three years, maybe longer."

I admire their spirit of adventure, as well as the unscheduled nature of their trip. There are new levels of "unplanned" I can aspire to.

I have taken my first big risk to make contact with strangers and the results are encouraging for this newbie pilgrim.

Contrasted with our first *refugio*, Roncesvalles hosts pilgrims in a style I can only describe as "industrial-strength," housing 120 people in one giant room full of 60 two-tier bunk beds. The dormitory arrangement is unexpected, especially after last night. I'm too overwhelmed to bring out my poetry book. However, one of the elements I find particularly amusing this night is the soundscape of night-time pilgrims; an incredible symphony of snoring from all around me. I keep wishing I had an audio recorder.

Shared dormitory, sleeping bodies, multicultural snoring, male and female alike:

French: *ronfler*
Spanish: *roncar*
Hungarian: *horkolás*
German: *schnarchen*
Danish: *snorke*
Dutch: *snurken*
Italian: *russare*

Portugese: *roncar*
Croatian: *hrkati*
Finnish: *kuorsaus*
Norwegian: *snorke*
Swedish: *snarkar*
And on and on into the long night.
I laugh myself to sleep at the variety of snoring sounds
that can be produced by human beings.

CHAPTER 5

A day of mostly elevation loss.

Our walk today has a section called The Enchanted Forest, and it lives up to its name. Even though it rains off and on throughout the day, my spirits remain high. The trail is muddy, the kind of sticky clay that clings to my boots, but because we are on a downhill, my progress isn't slowed down much. This landscape—the footpath sheltered by pine trees as it winds through uplifted grey shale—reminds me of hiking in Kananaskis Country outside of Calgary. The scent of pine in the air is refreshing and I feel so alive.

We keep encountering familiar faces. Each time we meet, we adjust our pace to walk in synchrony as we share information about where we're from, how long we've been walking, and what prompted our journey. So far we have met people from Australia, Germany, France, Netherlands, South Korea, and one other couple from Canada. Oh yes, and England. There are many British pilgrims on the route. During the day, Rod and I practice our Spanish, rehearsing the kinds of questions we'll need to ask, and possible answers we'll receive. Many of our questions start with, "*Donde esta* ...." Where is ....? We have to be prepared for an answer delivered at warp speed, not always understanding what is being said. Practising together is a great way to pass the time. Russell doesn't speak Spanish, so he's often lost in the mix of languages we are hearing on the trail. He's drawing on the limited French he learned in high school. Survival Spanish: What are the most basic elements he needs to know? While my most important phrase is, *"Donde esta el baño,"* Russell concentrates on learning how to order the food and drinks he wants.

> *"Un café con leche por favor."* [A coffee with milk please.]

> *"Una cerveza."* [A beer.]

> *"Para mi primero, me gustaria …."* [For my first course, I would like …]

He's a smart person, he's resourceful, and I trust he'll learn as much as he needs to on this journey.

Our arrival in Zubiri is somewhat of a let-down. People do not smile on the street here as they have in other places. The landscape is grey, torn up by the magnesium plant that sits on the edge of town. I wonder what effect that plant has on the people who live here. It reminds me of the work I do back home, where I interview Indigenous Peoples, asking them to describe how development on traditional lands will affect or has affected the ability to carry out customary activities: hunting, fishing, gathering berries and medicines, conducting ceremonies, travelling to harvesting areas. My heart breaks when I hear individuals speak of the destruction of a way of life.

"Back in the day, when it was springtime and the birds would come back, there was music and colour in the forest. So much life all around me. Now? There is no music, all the birds are gone. We just have crows and ravens."

Frustrated voices speak: "The animals are gone. All that noise around here has scared them away. Now we have to drive for miles to find just one moose. It used to be we could walk outside our door and find a moose in half a day. We need that meat to be healthy."

I hear how quiet time in nature is essential to well-being, about a treasured point of land on the lake where ancestors first chose to settle, where the people have gone for healing for generations. I hear descriptions like, "That's a really special place. The river flows out where our campsite is, and my grandpa is buried there. When I need to make a decision, I go out there for three or four days, all alone. I talk to grandpa and the other old ones. I come back home knowing what I need to do next." I hear that peace and quiet is rare now. "With all the companies working around us, it's noisy all the time. They keep lights on at night, so there's no more dark sky. I can't see the stars anymore."

My work requires me to ask questions like, "How do you feel when you hear that a company wants to build on that piece of land?" As much as I hate voicing these words, it's worse to hear the pain and grief in the answers I receive. "It's not right." "Angry." "This place is like our church. Would you tear down a church to build a (fill in the blank)?" I see tears on weathered faces, damp handkerchiefs in balled-up fists. "What about my grandchildren, what's going to be left for them?" I see the shock on faces when people recognize what specific lands will be converted into a construction zone. "That's my fridge." "That's my backyard."

So it's not hard for me to imagine what the people here in Zubiri are feeling. Were there residents who wanted the industrial development and others who resisted? Did that leave a divide in the community? Are they shocked at how much the valley has changed since the mine started operating? Has the economy improved the way the company promised? This is such a small scale development compared to what I have seen in northern Alberta, and yet the torn-up land feels familiar.

As does the sensory impressions of pain, disconnection, and the lack of spark and joy in people's eyes here.

Even the *refugio* dormitory doesn't look very attractive to us when we go to check in, so we find a pension with a room for the three of us. It's been a grey, wet day, and now we're in a grey wet town, so it's a reprieve to be out of the rain in a more private space. We eat in the nearest restaurant and choose from the *Menu del Dia* options. I consider this to be the Pilgrim Menu since it's the least expensive. If we're not going to prepare our own food, we have to find ways to spend as little as possible. As we eat, we don't pay much attention to the food. Instead we are preoccupied by making a list of the equipment we need to look for when we get to Pamplona tomorrow. Russell has decided he needs hiking poles. He's changed his mind about not using them on this journey after just two days. I have no regrets about bringing hiking poles along; I'm glad I added the rubber tip protectors so I can walk more quietly on the pavement and cobblestones. I'd dearly love to silence the clacking of Rod's poles as he walks along, but it's now become a sound I allow to fade into the background most of the time.

I need a battery charger for my camera, with an adapter for Spanish electrical plug-ins. I was so sure that because Rod and I have the same brand of camera, we could share the same charger. I didn't check before we left Calgary. I was wrong. Not even our battery chargers are compatible.

Tonight, with just the three of us in one room, I pull out Billy Collins and again choose a poem at random. I open the book to "Where I Live" and read out loud. There is a strange perfection in the poem, fitting for this time and place. I don't ask whether Russell and Rod want to listen.

I just want to hear the sound of my voice without having to reveal the sadness in my heart and the darkness in my mind. Like that torn-up land, there is no music or colour in me tonight.

CHAPTER 6

APRIL 21, DAY 3
ZUBIRI TO PAMPLONA
(21 KM)

Once again, the landscape is decidedly pastoral. Late in the morning we need to take a break from our walking while a flock of sheep is herded through one of the small villages on the route, leaving no room for anyone else to pass by. We are steadily dropping out of the highest section of our Camino; although we're still in the foothills of the Spanish Pyrenees today could be one of our last days in this terrain. Sheep continue to dot the hillsides, their mostly white coats standing out against the green grass. Occasionally there are small herds of cows, and even less frequently ponies are visible in the open fields. These cleared areas are bordered by forest, so I'm reminded of patchwork squares on a quilt. A few animals amidst the herds of cows and sheep wear bells that clang in different tones, adding a layer of sound to this landscape. I often hear the bells before actually seeing the flock, and it's a sound that's pleasant to my ears. Sheep bells have a higher tone than those worn by cows because they are smaller. Animal bell chimes. Has anyone ever tried to tune the bells on a flock so they create chords or scales?

I'm surprised that so much of the Camino route involves walking on narrow paved roads, leading from village to village. The vehicle traffic isn't too heavy, thank goodness, and I'm often surprised when I hear the sound of an engine grinding up a hill behind me. It's a reminder that there are people who live and work here, that there's a rich rural life going on day-to-day while we move through with packs on our backs. So far the locals we've met have been very gracious, even respectful of us as pilgrims. We seem to have a special status as we walk along these footpaths and roadways.

Along the unpaved pathways, spring flowers at the ground level have been grabbing my attention. Today it was hard to miss the large patches of showy purple gentians, nestled in among the rocky edges of the trail. I've never seen such colourful displays of deep purple trumpets clustered low to the ground. In the Canadian Rockies, gentians are quite rare and much smaller. Small buds are forming on many plants and shrubs, awaiting their turn to command the attention of the passers-by. The trees have not yet leafed out but hints of green are showing on the tips of their branches. Looking over the distance, there is evidence of new life that grows more visible each day.

There is also plenty of evidence that we are in Basque country, with slogans on building walls proclaiming, "Freedom for the Basque Country!!!!" That one in English. I am able to decipher one written in Spanish: "País Vasco no es España". [Basque Country is not Spain.] I suspect that the other messages written in the Basque language have a similar sentiment. The road signs indicate distances to unpronounceable village names like Ilurdotz and Antxoritz. These names inevitably remind me of the Asterix and Obelix comics I used to read with Russell and Emma when they were younger. As I pass through this landscape, I realize that those comics captured much of the history and attitudes of people who have resided here for hundreds, perhaps thousands, of years. I wish I could teleport Emma to this section of the Camino so she could walk with us along roadways, reading unpronounceable names. I want to hear her impressions of this rural countryside, and what memories arise in her. I'd like her to know how much I miss her in this moment.

My meandering mind is brought back to the here and now as we arrive at a small park-like space with a few picnic tables scattered under large trees. It's an inviting scene. We choose a table to eat our simple lunch of bread, meat and cheese. Sebastian and Norman from Cologne join us at the table. It becomes obvious they don't have much food, so we share what we have. They gratefully accept and after we eat, entertain us in return. Norman pulls out his juggling clubs. A small group gathers around him as Sebastian starts to sing and they begin their routine. The energy is contagious, and the audience begins to clap along with the song. They bow and sit down, accepting the coins being offered. As the crowd dissipates, I pull out Billy Collins and randomly choose a poem to read aloud. "Afternoon with Irish Cows." I love the rhythm and cadence of the words. The two German pilgrims don't fully understand what I've said, and it doesn't matter. I've shared something of me in this moment.

As we pack up to leave, Sebastian and Norman tell us, "We're going to catch the bus into Pamplona."

I protest. "Why are you doing that? That's not what pilgrims do!"

"Why not?" they ask with smiles on their faces.

"Well," I say, "pilgrims are supposed to walk everywhere. It's like cheating if you take a bus."

"Pick up this pack," directs Norman. I try, and can barely lift it. "This one has my juggling clubs. Now you know why we're taking a bus. See you in Pamplona."

We separate from the two buskers at a bus stop, as Rod, Russell and I continue walking. We are each absorbed in our own worlds. No conversation is necessary. This quiet time is very different than the "silence as a weapon" my mother practiced while I was growing up.

*   *   *

I am ten or eleven years old. My older sister, Annette, is fifteen or sixteen. Our mother thinks that the worst thing that could happen to one of her daughters is to get pregnant. "I know what you're up to," she accuses Annette. "I know what you're up to" is what I hear when I've spent a long time in the bath. Does she know that I've discovered that private place in my body where I can give myself pleasure? I'm not going to confess that secret to her. Thankfully the spotlight is more on Annette, since she's fighting constantly with Valentine about curfew hours, about who she's dating, and her clothing choices. Annette has defiantly started wearing mini-skirts and blue jeans to school.

Dad's away from home again. We four younger kids and Mom are all home for lunch when another outburst happens.

"You're not going to school dressed like that!"

Val's voice screams and her hand grasps the nearest object to her that resembles her licken stick. It's a toy sword, quite sturdily made, with a silver handle and a flat blade. Mom starts whacking Annette on her back and legs, hard. I freeze and hope the beating stops soon. I wish I couldn't hear. Thwack! Thwack! This goes on for several minutes as Annette yells back.

"I'll wear whatever I want to! You're such a bitch!"

"You should be ashamed of yourself, wearing those short skirts. The boys are going to get the wrong idea about you. You're just asking for trouble!"

Annette doesn't flinch, no matter how hard Mom hits her, no matter how harsh her accusing words are. I love Annette for standing up to Mom, but there's no way I would ever tell her. I don't want to be seen taking sides with the current outsider in our family.

Hitting and loud voices stop. It's time for us to go

back to school. Annette leaves with the rest of us, sullen; we don't talk to each other at all. Annette doesn't come home for the next three nights. The house feels empty and cold to me. When she does come back she doesn't speak to Mom. Neither does Valentine attempt to speak to Annette. They seem determined to maintain silence, neither one willing to be the first to speak. Their refusal to talk to each other goes on for many weeks; finally my father intervenes and pressures my sister to break the impasse. True to form, when my mother chooses to speak with Annette again there is no resolution of any kind, no explanation given. We carry on as if nothing unusual has happened.

*   *   *

I emerge from this remembering, suddenly aware that I also impose silent treatment on those around me. I've been withholding myself in silence on this trip without even realizing it, especially in the ways I choose to say nothing to Rod. Even when my head is full of images and impressions I long to share with someone. And why not my husband? Or even Russell?

Then I fall back into memory.

*   *   *

I do almost anything to avoid being the target of Valentine's shunning. I have learned to sense the rising, sharp-edged energy that signals my mother's anger is building. These times feel like a thunderstorm, not on the horizon, but inside our family home, the classic anvil clouds forming with her flat-edged sentences, then lighting flashing as her eyes spark and dart around the room, and finally, the booming thunder of her anger-filled accusations. Most of my mother's touch was in the form of punishment. Explosions happened with surprising ferocity, like the time my mom leaped up from the dinner table, grabbed a frying pan and hit one of my older brothers on the head with it. I think that was to "hit home" her point that he wasn't working hard enough at school. The rest of us kept our eyes down, continuing to eat. In silence. My brother sat stoically, refusing to show any signs of injury.

Whenever I come home from school, I cautiously enter the house from the carport, sliding open the door into our mudroom. This is where our washer and dryer are, with a large closet for hanging jackets and a sink for hand-washing clothes. I slip off my jacket as quietly as possible, peek into the kitchen, testing the atmosphere. Where is my mother? What is she doing? How does she greet me? Or not. Based on what I notice, I might make myself scarce. Or hang out at the kitchen table with her, sociable and chatty. We've got a built-in bench around the large table, big enough to hold at least six bodies. Sometimes mom will offer Red Rose tea and toast as a snack; it's one of her favourites. Maybe I'll quietly make cookies as a way to bridge the frozen silence hanging around my mother. The worst times are when Mom is ironing clothes in our laundry room, the common entrance to our house. Mom + ironing = REALLY PISSED OFF MOM. Translation: *I'm going to get beat up.* Once I've opened the door onto that mother, there's no escape.

*   *   *

I emerge from this reverie at the outskirts of Pamplona. It takes a long time to get to the centre of the city where the *refugio* we plan to stay at is located. Pamplona buildings are attractive although it seems as if garbage collection is not a high priority. The rank odours of rotting food and who knows what else keep us moving along at a fast clip. I don't have a good sense of smell but even I'm on the edge of nausea until we leave that unpleasantness behind.

We check in at the *Jesus y Maria refugio*, which has space for 120 people. The *hospitalero* is an older woman who greets us warmly as she stamps our *Credencial* and assigns us to our bunk beds. This building is actually an old church that has been recently renovated to accommodate pilgrims. There are many thoughtful touches here, including a well-stocked library with comfortable chairs to sink into. I browse the shelves and select an obscure title written in English. After I've enjoyed the padded comfort of one of these chairs, I continue to wander. Free laundry facilities are tucked away in the back, so we take full advantage. One load of washing at last night's pilgrim hostel would have cost a prohibitive six euros. I laugh to myself, as we never fill more than one load of laundry with all of our clothing combined. I'm always on the lookout for ways to save money.

Each numbered bunk bed has an adjacent numbered cupboard for storing a pack and other gear. We discover a large kitchen upstairs, along with a common area for sitting and visiting for those who so desire. But not for us. Boots come off, packs get stuffed out of sight, and we're off to the shops. Russell is on a search for hiking poles; I'm hoping to find a camera battery charger. It gives us a reason to roam the streets and take in the sights. I'm impressed with how easily we find the stores that sell what we need. The *hospitalero* at *Jesus y Maria* gave us very good directions.

Practical tasks done, we continue to wander through the historic city core. There are beautiful clothes in the shop windows and enticing displays of food in the markets. However we are not easily seduced, given we have to carry everything we buy. Instead we carry on exploring, and stumble upon the site of an old fortress, which is now a park. It's on a hill, overlooking the rest of Pamplona. Emma would love this place. If only we could transport her here. I imagine Emma wandering through these ruins steeped in history, making up stories for us about medieval dinner parties, describing what would typically be served at a meal, everyone eating without utensils. She might invite us to try a "no-utensils night" on the trail, like we did one night while Rod was away from home on an archaeology field trip.

As I walk in silence I imagine the letter I would write to Emma if I were, right at this moment, at a desk with pen and paper:

Although you aren't here with us, Emma, you are very much present to me. I imagine you exclaiming over the stonework, fascinated by the architecture. I've always been amazed by you, by how your mind is so able to analyze how things work, how buildings are constructed, and how you can talk with Rod so easily about all those details he's got stored in his brain. While I drift off, the two of you can talk for long hours about "how things work." And at the same time, your mind has that capacity for imagining and fantasy, able to see the absurd in the ways I do. Like looking down into the green spaces that are part of the fortress complex, amused by the assortment of animals there. Deer. Peacocks. Chickens. We'd laugh together at this bizarre collection, in Pamplona, Spain, understanding each other whether we're in Canada or elsewhere.

I look forward to getting to each refugio, hoping to find an Internet connection so I can send you updates from along the way. I love receiving messages from you, my young-old wise daughter. My friends have often pointed out that you have wisdom beyond your years. An "old soul." You were always interested in potions and spells and fairies that lived under our crab apple tree in the back yard. You and your friends would gather in the big spruce tree in Morgan's yard, creating magic together. I bought you books and crystals and signed you up for classes exploring feminine energy, developing girl-power. I wanted you to know you were supported, even if I didn't understand your ways. I wanted you to have something different from what I grew up with.

I still don't feel comfortable in my female body and I was never certain what I could do as your mother to support you to love your physical self. I did my best to provide opportunities for you that allowed you to spend time with other girls and women, sharing your experiences and moving through rites of passage together. I looked for female-only events that attracted me and asked if you wanted me to sign you up, gatherings that may have filled the void I felt when my body started to change with puberty. It seems to me from this vantage point that I was making decisions based on what I didn't want to repeat. Was that what you wanted?

I imagine you would enjoy this journey if we were traveling at a different pace, tackling shorter distances. I suspect you would want to use taxis to transport your pack to the next town or, on tougher days, use transportation other than walking to move on to the next stage. When we walk through a section of a town that has especially intriguing features, or we're sitting in a café with aromatically appealing, mouth-pleasing baked treats, I picture you so clearly, eating meals that take us a long time to consume, with all the different courses. Taking time to talk, and really listen to each other. These are Emma moments.

If you were here, Emma, you might soften some of the edges that have been appearing between Rod and Russell, as the two of them sometimes interact as if they are in an academic sparring match. One-up-man-ship about who knows the most about European history. Who knows more about Roman architecture, the purpose of art in culture, and the history of art? Who's the best at reading a map and navigating? Russell will start out by saying, "When I was in my first year Art History class, I learned how art tells a lot about culture as a whole." I'm intrigued by Russell's analysis and want to hear more. Rod, on the other hand, likes to change the topic. "You know the Romans were the first to build with arches." This subtle power struggle feels like a clashing of swords and I don't want to be caught in the middle. I'd love to have you here as my female ally, Emma.

I report my observations about Rod and Russell to Emma in my next email update. The rest of this imagined letter feels important enough for me to wait and share with her in person.

As much as I long for female companionship, Emma is not physically here. So I return mentally to where I am, walking and observing the two males beside me. I think what I'm witnessing is the shifting power in the father-son relationship. From what I can see, it's not comfortable for Rod to have his son assert more of his opinions or to be well-versed in a topic like art history. Who has the best ideas? Who decides?

To top it all off, Rod still does his usual I-won't-say-what-I-want routine. Last night Russell and I were about to go into a restaurant that looked appealing to us.

Rod declared, "This one won't be good for Russell."

Russell called him out. "This is bullshit. I can speak for myself and this place seems fine to me."

Rod stomped off in a huff. We followed. It took us a long time to find another restaurant. Not surprisingly, my appetite was low after that episode, and I didn't eat much. When the tension builds and outbursts occur, I end up feeling extremely unsettled. My biggest fear is that I'll be left alone, that somehow, I'm not worth having in our party of three. It's crazy thinking, I know, but that fear is lodged in my brain. These past few days Rod has refused to hear much about what's going on for me emotionally. It's like he's heard enough, and he's tired of my ups and downs. My reactions have been to lash out in anger or retreat into silence. I'd dearly love to find some middle ground, where I could communicate something about what's going on inside without feeling so threatened or unwelcome.

Travelling together like this brings out the best and the worst in me. I'm surprised by how quickly I move into resentment, especially when I hear a familiar and irritating pattern of response one more time. Like Rod not saying what he really wants, but framing it as a question, "Do you want to eat over here?" Or the times he asks, "Where do you want to eat?" and when I give an answer, he inevitably wants something very different than what I suggest. But he won't speak up first. After all our years together, it's those patterns that feel like sandpaper to my psyche, my desire for a direct response rubbing up against Rod's elusive style.

Finally, it's time to head over to the restaurant we've chosen for the evening. Following Spanish protocol, it doesn't open until eight o'clock so my hunger level is high by the time we are seated. While late for our usual supper time, it's still early for the locals. I'm already looking forward to a fresh green salad, with spring greens, goat cheese with grated carrots, and light vinaigrette. So far the only salads I've encountered have been potato or pasta based with a lot of mayonnaise. Combined with the bread for breakfast and lunch, my carb intake is higher than I expected. This is a source of anxiety for me. *I'm going to gain weight on this trip* is another constant internal refrain.

I do get to order that green salad I'm craving, along with calamari and dipping sauce. Rod orders lamb with potatoes and veggies on the side. It's a large platter and his eyes light up with glee when his dish arrives. Russell has pork ribs along with seasonal vegetables. This meal is great for hungry carnivores. The obligatory bottle of red wine starts out our evening, and we slowly consume our several courses.

Even though we're stuffed, we finish up with dessert, something we don't normally have at home. Tonight, it's a flan. After all the walking I've done, I don't hold back on my consumption. I try to resist, but more often than not my plate is as empty as the guys' when the waiters come by to clean up. I hate myself for not having more self-restraint. It's a constant struggle between giving in to hunger, indulging in what is on the menu, and suffering emotionally because much of this food is on my "no-no" list.

I'm an anxious pilgrim; I didn't expect food to be such a challenge. But then again, when hasn't it been?

CHAPTER 7

APRIL 22, DAY 4
PAMPLONA TO PUENTE LA REINA
(24 KM)

It's a long way from the centre of Pamplona to the outskirts, a pleasant walk without the smell of rotting food and dirty diapers that greeted us on our way into the city. There are increasing numbers of pilgrims walking the route and we're all following the scallop shell markers. On the way out of town, Russell spots a sign, *University of Navarra, pilgrim stamp here.* Russell and I are both keen to collect extra stamps for our *Credencial*, while Rod is reluctant. He trails along in the wake of our enthusiasm. Signs on the university campus direct pilgrims to the administration building and as we enter, a well-dressed man in a grey suit recognizes the Canadian Company of Pilgrims crest on Rod's pack. He rushes over to us, wanting to engage in conversation.

"You are Canadians, are you not?"

"Yes, we are."

"And you are pilgrims?" It is both a question and a statement.

"Yes, we're on our way to Santiago."

We quickly find out that, although this man is originally from Canada, he has lived in Spain for thirty-nine years. He is now head of the geography department at this university, and he's hiked the Camino several times.

"I have written books about the pilgrimage."

His voice is full of emotion as he speaks about the magic of the Camino. Glancing at his watch, he says, "I would love to take you for coffee and hear about your experiences. The Camino—ah, it is such a special journey. But I have a class to teach that starts in ten minutes. You must come back another time."

"Yes, we will come back."

As we are leaving, Russell says, "He's part of the Camino magic." I couldn't agree more. I feel an out-of-proportion, child-like glee at receiving a *Credencial* stamp, at our unexpected encounter, and the generous welcome this professor extended to us. As we walk out of the campus, I imagine myself returning to Pamplona. In my silent moments, I create a whole new life for myself, fluent in Spanish and working at the university among new friends. Rod is somewhat disgruntled by our choice to take the extra time just to get a stamp, and lets us know by his huffy silence. It's like the magic had no effect on him.

We walk out of Pamplona and enter a vineyard-covered countryside. Now that we have dropped down from the high country, we are moving through well-tended rows of grapes, olive trees, and almond trees, set against the backdrop of red soil. The grape vines have been pruned back, and it's hard to believe they will be producing anything by the end of the season. It's still early spring and the leaves have yet to appear. This landscape is full of a rich, earthy nuance; cliffs display various hues of red, orange and brown. The colours of Spain speak to my heart.

Mountains have now been replaced by hills. Off in the distance we can see the church spire from the next village on the route. Every village and town seems to have a church on a high point, visible for miles around, associated with a central square and a public fountain to refill water bottles. I check our guidebooks regularly to see what places along the way have services for pilgrims and our day unfolds in a series of slow-moving vignettes.

Although the clouds are low for most of the morning

and into the early afternoon, there is no rain today. By the time we stop for lunch at *Alto el Perdon*, a high point of land, the clouds part and we are bathed in sunlight. I'm ready to bask in the sun. After chomping down our usual lunch fare of whole-grain bread, sliced spicy salami, and sheep's milk cheese, we take a longer break than usual, giving our feet and backs a rest. As I relax with my back against a large rock, bare feet free of boots and socks, I enjoy the luxury of dessert, tart green apples we picked up in one of the Pamplona markets. Everything about this day seems to signal *take time to enjoy*. Our next stop is a café a short distance away where I order *café con leche*—half coffee, half milk—along with a croissant. Who knew that Spain had great croissants? The flaky buttery half-moon fuels the rest of my walk. Like every treat I've indulged in so far, it was worth the extra calories. We stop again in Obanos, lounging in the plaza adjoining the stone church until we mobilize once again.

From Obanos it's a short distance to Puente la Reina, our destination for the day. On that final section we walk along with an international party of four men: one each from France, Greece, Mexico, and Germany. Fortunately, they speak enough English for us to have conversations about where we're from, why we're on the trail, and how we have structured our lives in order to do this long walk.

Vasili from Greece tells me, "I inherited my parents' house after they both died. I live on the rental income as I travel the world. I am very frugal in my habits, so my money goes a long way." I feel a wisp of envy rise at the freedom he's created for himself.

I say to Rod, "Let's sell everything and walk."

He replies, "I need a home!" My fantasy world crashes.

I am finding it easier to start conversations with the new people I meet every day. I notice how quickly I form attachments. I miss seeing familiar faces I've gotten to know in this short time on the trail. I imagine this will be the nature of our encounters, forming and re-forming a community of pilgrims. Already we are assigning names to individuals and groups we are meeting throughout our days. There is the crowd we call the Italian Soccer Team, who are very loud while they walk, love to drink and party when they've stopped, and still seem to effortlessly cover the miles. There's the German Drinkers with a Walking Problem, older husbands who are happily consuming much wine as they make their way across northern Spain. A pilgrimage is the only reason they could give their wives for such a long time away from home. They seem to take great pleasure in this journey, particularly at the *refugios*. I'm always amazed at how many wine bottles end up at their table. Then there are the French Purists, who have an air of religious superiority about their walk and often seem to exude a sense that the rest of us are not doing it right. I have wondered what our name might be.

As we enter Puente de la Reina, the four men peel away from us, heading toward the first hostel on the edge of town.

"Come with us," they call.

We resist. My Confraternity of Saint James guidebook describes this *refugio* as "basic and busy." I'd like to find a more peaceful home for the night, with at least a few creature comforts. I read a description for the *Albergue Santiago Apostol* which reads: "hot showers, washing machine and dryer." I'm drawn to simple amenities now. We trudge through town on our way to the *albergue,* then cross the Roman bridge constructed of stones, named *Puente de Peregrinos,* to get there. I'm pleased to see there are fewer people staying here since it's further from the centre of town.

Once we settle in, we meet the others staying here. Some pilgrims have taken on a legendary status and I've been wondering if they really exist. Here in this *refugio* I finally meet the Australian Family we've heard so much about, several generations travelling together. There is the grandfather who travels by taxi ahead to the next stage. Younger grandchildren who don't feel like walking that day join him in the taxi. The Australian Family grandmother is still fit and well enough to keep up with her adult children and their partners on the trail. Family members who choose to walk carry small daypacks, since the rest of their gear is sent on ahead in the taxi. We hear that other family members will be joining the group as they get closer to Santiago. They form a large, boisterous, joyful crowd, and I absorb the energy of a group that obviously enjoys being together. We sit around the large kitchen table, sharing stories about our journey so far, where we're from, how far we walk each day. It's a treat for me to spend time in conversation with others, to break out of my cloud of silence and the patterns of interaction within our party of three.

In our usual fashion we wander into town before supper, once again walking over the Roman bridge spanning the Arga River. There are two churches in this town, so we take time to enter each, noting some of the different architectural features. I don't feel the same level of reluctance entering buildings of religious worship that I did at the beginning of our travels. There is much devotion contained within the building walls. I'm not sure why but it seems a personal loss if I refuse to enter. A church or large cathedral usually marks the end of each stage of walking, so it can also be a relief to enter and sit down in a peaceful place.

After just a few days on the trail, my resistance is shifting to intention. Maybe this pilgrim stuff is getting to me. Whatever baggage I am carrying about the Catholic religion, I feel a change going on inside. I decide to enter each building with appreciation for what is before me, without my cynicism taking over. Instead of focusing on the enormity of the structure, the opulence of the altars, or any of the historical background that provokes my negative judgment, I search for something beautiful. My curiosity inevitably leads me to the alcoves and side chapels housing statues of different saints placed around the perimeter of each building, well away from the main altar. Not surprisingly, many cathedrals I have entered so far have chapels devoted to Saint James. I prowl the church, searching for alcoves dedicated to Saint Anthony or Saint Francis. Then I follow my simple routine of asking for blessings and well-being, a practice I began in the Basilica of San Sernin. I do this by lighting candles provided for this purpose, near the base of the saint's statue. Candles of different sizes are available for a small donation, ranging in price from one to ten euros depending on size. My requests are now inspired by my immediate needs.

Today, my request is: *Please make the cramps in my feet stop hurting so much so I can complete this journey.* My foot cramps started up on Day One and they haven't let up since. Every morning by eleven my feet are in agony and I have to find ways to distract myself from the pain. Sometimes I think about quitting.

It's a mystery to me how I can be here in a church lighting candles to a saint and asking for blessings. I hardly feel worthy of receiving what I ask for. This thought connects me to my mother in an instant.

Valentine went to a Catholic convent boarding school in northern Alberta, one of a few Caucasian youngsters among many indigenous children. She spoke little of her experiences there, most often making it sound like fun. She told the same few stories over again.

"I was so bad the nuns had to lock me up in the closet," she'd say with a girlish giggle.

"When I got my first period, the nuns held up my bloody panties and showed them off to the whole school. They hung them on the clothesline for the rest of that day."

"Sometimes we got into fights. We had to make sure the nuns didn't see us. If they did, we got the strap."

She remained a devout, fearful Catholic and our

family followed the Christian calendar under her strict leadership. She insisted that we attend church every Sunday, even when we were away on family holidays. Nothing felt stranger to me than having to brush the sand off our sun-baked bodies after a week at the beach, then drive to the local church in our "Sunday best." The grumbling in the car was intense but mom was fierce about not missing church services. During Lent, we gave up candy, said the rosary together as a family—without Dad—every evening, and went to early morning mass each day before going to school. I used to love going to the Midnight Mass at Christmas and at Easter. Regular masses, not so much. I started refusing to go to church when I was in my teens.

By then I craved an exciting life outside of the house that matched my inner world—wild and chaotic. The easiest route to that life was to take up drinking and smoking dope with a new group of friends. Once I started down that road I always had a crowd to hang out with. My behaviour at school deteriorated as I explored my new teenage persona. I was constantly lying about what I was thinking or doing to cover up the real me. Sometimes I'd get caught out in my stories, but it didn't stop me from telling tales to hide the truth. My resistance to my mother's rules was most often silent; I became sullen, doing my best to keep my face a blank mask.

My rebellion was in direct relation to how much I was hurting inside. The equation in our family was, "If you admit or show you are vulnerable, you will get hurt even more." For the most part, I chose to suffer in silence at home. I left the suffering behind for a while, in the haze of drugs and alcohol.

I circled back to religion in my late twenties. When Rod and I decided to get married in 1984, we chose to marry in the Catholic Church, mostly to honour our parents. We became active members of a faith community for a time, and both Russell and Emma were baptized in the church. However, as we kept hearing ongoing reports of abuse by Catholic priests, in churches and within the schools operated by various religious orders, in 1993 we once again stopped going. Although I had found more personal connection with others in that particular parish, and was participating in an active way, I still felt disconnected from myself as a spiritual being. My understanding of prayer seemed to be an academic exercise, limited to memorization and recitation.

More recently, I feel driven to look for the deeper meanings beyond the surface. Much of the time I don't know exactly what I'm looking for, but I'll know when I find it.

And now, on the trail, I continue to be curious about what it means to pray. When I light candles is that prayer?

I feel great nourishment when I am walking in nature. Is that prayer?

CHAPTER 8

APRIL 23, DAY 5
PUENTE LA REINA TO ESTELLA
(24 KM)

Last night Russell and I sat down to methodically map
out what the remainder of our trip needs to look like to
walk all the way to Santiago in the time that we have. It
was a humbling exercise, as we need to cover between
twenty-four and thirty-six kilometres a day for the next
twenty-six days. I hope I have it in me.

As we collect our packs and get ready to leave, the
Australians exclaim:

"How much does that weigh?" This is directed to me,
as I heft my 50-litre Gregory Deva onto my back.

"I have no idea, but it's manageable," I reply. "I love
this pack. It fits me like a hug." The Australians look far
from convinced.

"And you," they ask Russell, "how heavy is that pack?"

"Too heavy," he says with a laugh. There's truth in that
response. He's toting around a 70-litre pack. I'm grateful
the salesperson at Mountain Equipment Co-op directed us
against purchasing an even larger volume expedition pack
for this trip. Our packs are not filled to capacity but measured
against the tiny sacks that some people are carrying, we
look over-stocked. Rod says nothing, stoic as ever under
the weight of the gear in his 65-litre Gregory backpack.
From that point on, my curiosity is satisfied. Our Camino
name is the Canadian Family with the Heavy Packs.

Our walk to Estella starts out with a clear sky and low-lying fog which obscures some of the views. As the day warms up, the fog rises and visibility increases. Now we're walking through vineyards and almond groves that are gently sending out new leaves. We see hillsides with neat rows of grape vines, bare gnarly branches etched against the sky; fields edged with red poppies. I never tire of the red blooms, taking more pictures of poppies than is necessary. Those large red petals with the black stamens are so striking to my eyes, I want to fall into them. Perhaps I was a bee in another lifetime.

After some hours of idyllic walking, we enter a section of the Camino which parallels a major freeway. By mid-afternoon the temperature hits twenty-seven degrees Celsius. The heat drains our energy, slows our steps to a snail's pace. We stop for a cold drink around two-thirty and decide to take a siesta at the bar in the village of Villatuerta. I take a photo of the Exhausted Pilgrim, Rod sleeping at the outdoor café, skin reddening from the bright sun. Because of the impending sunburn, we wake Rod up to move into the shade, and get back on our way an hour later.

When we finally arrive in Estella—population of about 13,000—we make our way to the *San Miguel* parochial *refugio*, which is run by the Jacobeans, one of the many Friends of the Camino groups dedicated to pilgrim support along the route. We receive a warm welcome from the husband-wife team, along with a blessing:

May the sun bring you energy by day
May the moon softly restore you by night
May the rain wash away your worries
May the breeze blow new strength into your being
May you walk gently through the world and know its beauty all the days of your life.

I have been noticing a particular open-heartedness

among my fellow pilgrims; the ways we easily open up to each other and speak of our deepest longings and dreams as we share footsteps and conversation. I didn't know it was possible, but my heart cracks open even more as I hear this blessing. I feel as if I am reconnecting with my child-like innocence as I make my way to Santiago. It is so different than my usual day-to-day life, where I put on my emotional armour just to get through the day. The bigger the city, the more protection I require. I don't want others to see my vulnerability, to know anything about the way I hate the way my body looks, or how I'm constantly worrying about how much food I've eaten. I don't want anyone to know how scared I am, how anxious I get when I have to speak to people. When I have my armour on, I can pretend I'm normal. I think I've got most people fooled. Here on the Camino, the need for protection seems to be falling away.

This pilgrim hostel is *donativo*—meaning we stay for a donation rather than a set fee—with beds for up to thirty-six people (two rooms of eighteen each). The woman serves us a cup of tea once we've been assigned to our bunks, and invites us to join the shared supper being prepared by her husband. "He loves to cook. Every year we take our holidays so that we can serve in this *refugio*," she tells us. I continue to be inspired by the stories of service I'm hearing from the people who volunteer in the pilgrim hostels. We say yes to a home-cooked meal without asking what's on the menu. Once again, our entertainment after we have our tea and find out the meal time, is to go out into the city and explore on foot. I'm on the prowl for food items not readily available in the small *mercados* along the route. Peanut butter is top of my list. I'm so tired of eating dry crusty bread in the morning for breakfast, with only jam available. Well, sometimes there's butter too, but not often enough! When I've asked other pilgrims where I can buy peanut butter, most look at me like I'm from another planet. Seems to me this is a huge cultural divide between North Americans and Europeans. It's not stopping me! I am on a mission. In the first store I enter, I scan the grocery shelves, looking for that familiar label with the green background and the two oh-so-cute teddy bears looking right out at me, the Kraft symbol above their heads. I can hear the jingle in my head as I search: "Kraft, Peanut Butter, tastes fresher than peanuts—in the shell." Images of the two bears, Smoothie and Crunchy, are clear in my mind. No luck in store number one. We still have other items to pick up, so I check the shelves in each store I enter.

Finally, I score! I find a jar of the precious peanut butter I've been searching for, and although it's not a familiar label, I buy it gleefully without any of the anxiety I've been feeling about food purchases. By the end of this shopping spree we replenish our store of nuts and dried fruit for daytime snacks. We pick up fresh apples and oranges, cheese and meat for our lunch tomorrow. We find all of these and then, the *plato fuerte*. I find a specialty chocolate shop where I pick up a bar of thick, high-quality dark chocolate. We finish our shopping expedition at the town square, where we sit outside and enjoy a cold beer, spotting all the pilgrims coalescing at other tables surrounding the entire plaza. We review our purchases, engaging in conversations with a few others before making our way back to the *refugio San Miguel*.

During our time of sharing supper with the twenty-one others staying here, I end up sitting beside a fit-looking Irishman named James. He informs me he prefers to be called Jim. He's now living and working in London. His passion is running marathons, and he's planning to cover fifty kilometres a day on his Camino.

"I only have two weeks' holiday," he tells me. "I've already booked my flight out of Santiago."

I have no doubt he'll make his flight, once I hear his next sentence.

"The last time I took off from work was to run the

Sahara ultra-marathon," he goes on to say. "Every day we ran 42.2 kilometres—the length of a marathon—collapsed in our tents at the end of the day, got up and did it again. This was for five days straight."

"The Camino must seem like a cakewalk to you," I respond.

He smiles as he asks for seconds from the plate of roasted chicken being passed around the table. I reach for the bowl of salad that is beside the person sitting on the other side of me, trying to hide the fact that I am drawn into Jim's energy, feeling a little bit lustful. I remind myself to behave. Do pilgrims have affairs while they're walking with their husbands on the trail? Thank goodness Rod is sitting further down the table, engaged in conversation with two men from Germany who are describing their favourite wines.

I don't really know what Rod is thinking on this walk.

CHAPTER 9

APRIL 24, DAY 6
ESTELLA TO LOS ARCOS
(21 KM)

As we get ready to leave the *refugio* this morning, I choose the rose quartz stone to leave at the base of the Saint James statue in the entranceway. Rose quartz vibration is love, and I feel it everywhere in this well-cared for building. I hand forty euros to the *hospitalera*. She is shocked. "It is too much," she cries. My reply? "It's worth it!" I insist she takes the money and won't take anything back. But as I walk away, my mind is filled with questions about how much money I gave. Was it really too much? There were three of us, and we had a meal. My calculations seemed accurate and appropriate for the level of service. A simple thank you from her would have made the transaction feel complete. Instead I feel unsettled.

As I stand outside waiting for Rod, I'm prompted to wonder, *Do I do this in my daily life?*

What are the ways I push away what comes to me, saying or thinking, *It's too much. Oh no, you shouldn't have.*

It's the sort of response Valentine had, like the Christmas gift of a fur coat. "Oh Mike, you shouldn't have."

Am I like Valentine in this way?

Walking away from the *refugio* interrupts this train of thought. Just before we cross the old stone bridge over the Arga River, Jim overtakes us, pauses a moment to wish us well, and carries on. I watch his back departing into the distance as he takes long smooth strides that will easily cover the miles. I have some envious thoughts as I watch him cross the bridge and move out of sight. His movements are fluid and strong. His pack is tiny and I ponder how he manages to travel so lightly. I feel the edge of physical desire at the sight of lean leg and butt muscles working to propel him forward.

At the edge of the city, just before the trail returns to the forest, my day takes a darker turn. I hear a deep voice yelling loudly. Rounding a corner, we come upon a man beating his Labrador-retriever-sized dog with a large stick. The animal cringes and whines, but is held tight to its owner by a leash. At this point my heart is so open it begins to crack from the onslaught of violence and my tears begin to flow. I feel each blow as if to my own skin, and I am transported in an instant to a much earlier time in my life, coming home from school, greeted by my angry mother holding her favourite stick.

* * *

The harsh words from my mother's mouth keep hammering away like rocks, wounding with each hit.

"You are such a slob! Look at those grass stains on your pants again. Can't you keep anything clean?"

I steel myself to her verbal blows and it seems like the stony silence I maintain escalates Valentine's anger. She automatically moves to hitting me with her licken stick when I don't react in any way.

What am I supposed to do? I wonder wildly inside my impassive facade. Thoughts scramble over each other.

I fell when we were playing tag at recess. I'm scared!

I reach inside myself, numbing myself to all forms of pain.

Do your worst, Mom, I am not going to cry. You can't touch me.

That final thought launches me out of my body, even though my physical self remains behind. After what seems like an eternity the yelling stops and the hitting slows down. Behind my wall of numbness I can't allow myself to feel the incredible loneliness of this moment or the sadness I feel from this encounter. I breathe a resigned sigh, quietly, so as to avoid activating Valentine's fury again, and I wait. Mom returns to herself and notices the stick she is holding. As if it is too much for my mother to bear the realization that she has once again beat her daughter, she dismisses me with her usual refrain.

"Go change your clothes and clean your room."

* * *

When I come out of this memory place, I appreciate that in this moment I've got Rod and Russell here beside me. Both men are kind, willing to listen, and offer comfort in the form of hugs and solid presence. They may not fully understand why I'm so upset, and I don't really know myself. On this day of witnessing violence on the pilgrim trail, I think I'm bothered the most by my silence. I didn't say a thing as I walked by. Instead, I tried to make myself as small as possible, kept my eyes averted, and slid on by. I can rationalize to myself that I didn't have enough fluency in the Spanish language to say anything to the man, although I'm not sure I would have been brave enough anyway. His stick was rather large and so was he.

I feel like my mind is weaving a tapestry, bringing together threads from past and present. There are loose strands. What are my tears really about?

I don't have much time to ponder that question. About two kilometres out of Estella, we arrive at the *Fuente del Vino,* a tap dispensing free wine provided by *Bodegas de Irache.* We've been hearing about this wine fountain since we started our journey in Saint Jean. Even though I don't really want wine at ten o'clock in the morning, it seems a shame to refuse the generosity. Rod gets out his water bottle and joins the line-up of pilgrims waiting for their turn, shrugging his shoulders at Russell and me as we stand off to the side to wait for him. I choose to fill my water bottle with water instead. Russell and I comment on how different people behave.

"Look at the small woman, she just pushed her way to the front," Russell observes.

"Rod's still close to the back of the line. At this rate he'll take an hour to get to the fountain," I say.

Russell and I place bets on how long it will take for Rod to fill his water bottle and for us to return to the trail.

"Forty minutes," I guess.

"Twenty-five," counters Russell.

Russell wins.

We continue our walk, mainly through vineyard country with red dirt visible beneath the grape vines. The fields look well-cared for, although we seldom see anyone working. Sometimes we pass into wooded areas and the route becomes a dirt track. I relax most in these sections of forest and footpath. The rest of the time we walk on narrow roads with not much vehicle traffic.

When I enter the first church on our route today, I light a candle in front of the statue of Saint Francis of Assisi for all the animals who need protection, who might be suffering right now. It is one small way to begin healing from the pain I carry from this morning's encounter. Healing also comes from walking into spring, from observing my surroundings, and noticing the small changes that are happening day by day. The greening of the forest trees, with leaves that are now visible rather than just a faint green haze in the distance. Flower buds forming, giving me an indication of what is to come. I imagine a shower of vibrant pinks and purples waiting to burst forth. The smell of the air changes, depending on where we are. Sometimes it is fragrant with the smell of flowers and the sap that is beginning to run in the trees.

In addition to stopping at the wine fountain, we also take advantage of the Spanish *panaderias*, sampling the baked goods, occasionally refuelling in the coffee bars that line the Camino. This is a whole new way of travelling and I am loving the rhythm of walking, choosing where to stop based on how we're feeling, and letting our energy levels determine how long we linger or how quickly we move down the trail.

It takes most of the day to recover my sense of equilibrium.

I ask Russell, "How did that man beating the dog this morning affect you?"

He looks me in the eye and says, "That was harsh. I don't like witnessing violence and I didn't know how to react."

I tell him, "You know, one of the reasons I was so upset is because my heart is so open right now. It's as if I was absorbing the pain of the dog while being reminded of my own pain as a child."

Russell is quiet for a while and then he says, "You know, it's important to accept that as much as there is beauty in this world, there is darkness too."

He's right. All I have to do is read the news on the Internet to see the latest deaths in Afghanistan, hostage takings, abductions, and the usual information that passes for news in our culture. It's so easy to feel removed from all that on our Camino journey, where the pilgrims I encounter, and the locals, seem so welcoming and open, willing to accept whoever is on the trail.

My thoughts turn again to my daughter at home, as I begin another imaginary letter to her:

Emma, I don't quite know how to describe this to you, but I keep generating an inner violence that seems out of place here. Resentment and anger accompany much of my walking. I hold bitter thoughts inside without speaking, which affects my whole day. My body feels like it's full of an emotional infection. My anger and resentment seem as out of place here as the man hurting his dog. Do you have any suggestions for your mother?

CHAPTER 10

APRIL 25, DAY 7
LOS ARCOS TO LOGRONO
(28 KM)

Packing up this morning, I wonder about what I should keep and what to send ahead to myself in Santiago. It's so hard to let go, even though I know the weight I'm carrying makes covering distances that much harder over the long haul. I'll have to make my choices tonight after supper, since tomorrow we will arrive in Najera where there's a post office. Mailing our belongings to Santiago is an option I read about and I want a lighter pack. I worry about having to speak in Spanish to negotiate sending a package by post. I remind myself that I've been making myself understood so far, and worry recedes to the background as I step out the door of our *refugio*.

The walk today continues through fields of wildflowers, along with what appears to be yellow canola in among the greening-up vineyards. Now that I have my camera battery charged again, I've been taking pictures of the more spectacular flashes of colour. Red poppies with their showy petals continue to line the paths and roadways we walk. I spot shrubs that look like forsythia to me, branches covered with yellow flowers before the leaves show themselves. Other vibrant yellow plants remind me of buckbean that I find on the prairie grassland in Alberta. One of the most striking to my eyes is a flower that grows very low to the ground, its petals a deep blue, perhaps a lobelia, although I don't know for sure. It's the deep blue that draws me in the most; the colour is so rich and the flowers so profuse it's hard to believe they haven't been planted by an over-zealous gardener. As we get closer to Logrono, we enter a zone of pink flowers emerging in full glory from larger shrubs that line the road, their blossoms overhanging the trail so that as we walk by, our heads are graced by the touch of soft petals. Without knowing their official names, I begin to assign my own, like these "pink blossom explosion bushes" that line this section of the Camino.

As I walk, I also observe the movements of numerous birds, although they often flit by so quickly I'm not able to do any kind of positive identification. I suspect that what I'm seeing and hearing are finches, sparrows, and flycatchers, mostly based on the behaviours I recognize from home. I'm quite certain I see swallows swooping and circling, their sharply angled wings familiar to my eyes. I love watching them as they form patterns in the sky during their morning feeding times. I hear the tapping of woodpeckers against tree trunks. Occasionally a hawk of some kind is soaring high above us as we plod along. And sometimes I hear a screech, before a hawk tucks its wings and goes into a dive, having found prey. I'm reminded of my childhood imaginings, of growing wings so I could fly.

My thoughts turned to you again, Emma, remembering you as a thirteen-year-old, fascinated with tropical ocean environments.

"I want to be a marine biologist," I heard you announce one day.

After the pronouncement you came up to Rod and me with a request, "Mom, Dad, can I paint my bedroom?"

"What do you have in mind?"

"I want to paint the ocean, with sea urchins, starfish, octopus, hammerhead sharks, kelp—all of it! And I'm going to do all the drawing and painting myself."

Rod and I looked at each other, skeptical. "Sounds like a lot of work. What if you just do one wall, like a feature wall?"

"No, I have to paint my whole room. I want to fall asleep and wake up as if I'm in the sea."

Rod and I weren't too excited about your plan to hand draw all the sea life, in addition to how much painting would be involved. So your Mom and Dad insisted on one blue wall, and you got to choose the paint.

"I like this one!" you said at the sight of an almost-electric tropical blue.

Together we chose a coral reef wallpaper strip to paste across the top of the wall. It seems a far cry from your original vision. Was that too much control over your very abundant imagination, Emma? I can't help but wonder how my responses to what I considered your wild ideas stifled your sense of who you are, who you could become, making it more difficult for you to step into being an adult.

As I return to my walking, one step in front of the other, I understand my mother better having raised my own daughter. Valentine seemed determined to stop my day-dreaming, to curb my creative fantasies. As a child I didn't understand why my mother would say things like, "Get your head out of the clouds." My imagination was so vivid, everything I had going on in my mind seemed as real as anything I could touch or feel.

Memories surface, pushing on each other like the water flowing downstream in a steep hillside torrent.

*   *   *

During the summers, I go down to the lakefront near our house. When there are no other kids to swim or play with, I amuse myself for hours tossing around an empty Coke bottle. I can still remember the curves on the bottle, and the grooves that make it easy to pick up and throw, the white Coke logo scrolled across the middle. I fill that bottle with enough sand to make it sink quickly, and toss it as far as I can. The game is that I can only swim underwater to retrieve it from wherever I have thrown it. I crawl along the sandy bottom of the lake to find my quarry. I become a deep-sea diver, swimming among coral reefs with brightly coloured fish around me, seaweed waving in the ocean currents. I have seen Jacques Cousteau documentaries, which ignite my vivid sense of the undersea world. I spend more time underwater than above, or so it seems, and if I keep at it long enough, another fantasy emerges, the one where I have gills, and I can breathe underwater without any special equipment at all. I am searching for buried treasure, a secret key to some special castle far away.

I have learned that I can't talk about any of the things that are happening to me. I don't have language for it. Mom gets mad at me; she can be really mean. I hear my parents fighting. I see my brothers and sisters getting hit and hurt by Mom and Dad. There are men who touch me where I don't want to be touched. That's just the way it is. Sometimes I feel a dark weight inside of me, like cold obsidian.

Chewing on the leg of my plastic doll. I'm very young, no more than four years old. I don't think I'm allowed to chew my doll. I'm angry about something, can't scream it out, so I chomp on that leg. It's an isolated, half-formed picture in my mind. I'm not sure what came before or after. I do remember the satisfying feeling of my jaws clamping down on the plastic, leaving teeth marks, feeling like I've ruined her somehow and that's good. Then a quick rush of fear that I might get caught, that I've done something bad.

Now I'm six years old. It's summertime, hot, and I'm feeling out of sorts. Bored, don't want to be in the house, no one to play with. What I really want to do is go swimming in the lake. Mom is too busy, no one else wants to take me there. My younger neighbour is sitting on the cement steps of the sidewalk leading up to her house. She's barefoot. So am I.

"Hey Susie, who gave you that popsicle?"

"My mom. I got to pick my favourite."

I pick up a large rock and drop it on her toes. Susie sets up a wail that startles me, "Mummmm! Marie hurt me!"

I want to run away, but Susie's mom is faster than I am. She grabs me by the shoulder, shaking me.

"I didn't do anything, it wasn't me!"

The whole time I feel completely disembodied as I watch myself pick up and drop the rock, shocked that I've done it, and still feeling like it wasn't me that did it. I'm telling the truth.

*   *   *

Returning to this present moment, I wonder if I'm still that hurtful person now, whether my parenting has somehow hurt my children, especially my very sensitive, caring daughter. Am I the reason Emma has spent almost two years sitting at a computer in the basement of the home she shares with B? Maybe I didn't know how to recognize my cruel words, my cruel body language. Will I ever have the courage to ask or hear the answer?

The unmistakable sounds of the cuckoo bring me

back to where I am on the trail, walking further away from Pamplona, moving deeper into the province of Navarre. The cuckoos serenade us all day long, calling from the forest and field margins. It's not a sound I want to bring into my home, the way some immigrants to Canada brought cuckoo clocks with them. It takes whatever willpower I have to shift from focusing on how much I would love those cries of "cuckoo, cuckoo" to stop. Rather, I put my attention elsewhere, anywhere.

I consider the preciousness of innocence and tears start to flow. I remember the way I felt each time I held my two newborn babies. First Russell, then Emma; I was struck by how they arrived so fresh and so clean. Knowing whatever the world was going to deliver, including how Rod and I would parent, would shape who they are as human beings. Those first few months of a baby's life involve so much trust and so much dependence on the quality of the caregiving. Even now, as I walk the Camino, I mull over how I may have let my children down, or was unavailable in ways that created wounding. I have wanted my children to have a life free of the pain I suffered while growing up.

It was helpful when a friend of mind, a wise parent, said to me, "Marie, no matter how well you parent, they will always have 'stuff.' The best you can do is pay for the counselling."

I gave up trying to be my version of the perfect parent, realizing I couldn't block out all the ways they might feel pain or hurt. That's just not possible. But, in my heart of hearts, if there was any way I could have kept them free from harm, I would have.

I recall times when, in spite of my best intentions, I feel the impulse to re-create my experience as a child so Emma and Russell will appreciate everything Rod and I are doing as Mom and Dad. Just one good licken so they know what is possible on the other side of how we treat them now. Then they might listen better. I might not hear them shout, "No!" or have to deal with their fights.

When I talked to Rod about having those feelings, all he said was, "Don't go there. That one time would do more damage than you can imagine."

So I keep taking deep breaths. Slowly counting 1...2...3...4...5. Giving myself space, sometimes locking myself in the bathroom just to be alone, collecting myself again, breathing. Finding a way to distract the kids. "Here, let's play with Lego." Or, "Do you want to play in the sandbox for a while?" Doing whatever it takes to keep myself from the hurtful impulses that vibrate within me.

It is most painful to understand that I—Marie the adult—am hungry for what my kids are getting from me. *What about me?* I ask myself. *Who's looking after me? How come they get all this good stuff, and I never do. It's not fair!*

It is like I am watching myself as I tend to my children, and the child-part of me is longing for respectful care, too. I see how innocent I was at the age of two, three, five, and seven, how vulnerable I was to preying adults, to harsh words and invasive treatment. My awareness hurts in a very deep way. How could my Mom do that? How could those men? Another wise counsellor told me, "Marie, it's impossible to make sense of the senseless."

That doesn't take away the pain.

When we arrive at Logrono and get close to the older city centre, we start looking for a store that carries equipment suitable for pilgrims. Russell needs a new pair of boots. He brought an older, broken-in pair of boots on the journey, but it turns out this was not a wise decision. We are hopeful that stores will be open and he can find something that fits. I'm also hoping that new boots won't be too hard on his feet while he goes through that breaking-in period so essential for most hiking boots. My son's feet are in bad shape. I get a glimpse of large puffed up blisters on his feet and I have to turn away.

Rod gleefully takes pictures of Russell's battered

feet, while I continue to avert my eyes. "What's wrong? This is good to have for the record."

Then Rod turns the camera onto his own feet which are covered in moleskin patches in his attempt to cushion the blisters on his toes and heels. He doesn't need new boots, but he's going through our first-aid supplies faster than I expected. Unlike Rod and Russell, I have no broken skin or hot spots on my feet. I have a different source of suffering; my feet go into spasm after walking two to three hours each day. The constant cramping and pain takes a toll on my sense of well-being. I waver between acceptance and anger as I walk along. My inner dialogue goes something like this:

Look for things that you are enjoying in this moment.

These fucking feet! I hate these cramps, they hurt so much.

What's something that has made you happy on this trip?

Dammit, Rod's ignoring me again. I am so tired of being invisible!

I need to blame someone, anyone, just to vent my outrage from constant pain. Rod is most often my target. Now *there's* a long-established pattern for me in relationship. I have been discovering a smouldering resentment directed toward Rod, for all the ways I believe he hasn't tended to my emotional needs. That energy resonates below the surface, a constant companion as I trudge along.

When we get close to city centre, we find an *albergue* in a down-in-the-mouth part of the city. The downtown area we explore also feels seedy, with a lot of cheap tourist souvenirs in every shop. I can't even find decent chocolate, which tells me a lot about the quality of everything else around here. So far I've been surprised by the availability of Spanish chocolate, even in some smaller towns. In fact, I've been thinking that I'd like to walk this route again, doing specific research for the guidebook on "best places to find great chocolate while walking the Camino." I think of myself as *The Chocolate Pilgrim* since I've been using dark chocolate to keep me going. When I'm losing steam, my feet hurting more than I can bear, wanting to quit, that's when I announce it's time for a break. I haul out my stash of precious dark squares, share them around, and feel my energy shift from despairing to hopeful. Maybe part of my spiritual quest is to discover more about the power of high quality chocolate.

Russell is at least able to find a decent pair of boots. He walks out of the store wearing them as our hunger propels us to find a place to eat in the central square.

There are a number of places to choose from surrounding the plaza. It's so hard to know which one might have the best food on offer, so we take a chance and walk into the corner restaurant, hoping that this location will be quieter. We're still looking for solitude, even in this city environment. I'm reminded once again that I'm in Spain as we enter this dimly-lit bar in Logrono. Not only by the sight of people smoking inside, whose burning cigarettes create a bluish haze, but also by the bullfight showing on the prominently displayed large-screen TV. *We're not in Canada anymore, Emma.* Scanning the other patrons sitting here, they're almost all men. Locals, by the looks of it. We've ended up in a bar where there are no other pilgrims. Is this a good sign, or not? It's not the sort of place I'd feel comfortable in on my own. Not that anyone else is even acknowledging me. All eyes are riveted on the bullfight. I've never been comfortable around groups of men who are smoking and drinking. Well, it's too late now, we're here, I'm hungry, and I'm sure there will be food of some kind for us to enjoy.

While we wait for our food orders to arrive my mind

meanders back to my childhood, to my grandfather, Cé, who was short and stocky, with a bald head and bushy moustache. He loved smoking strong cigars. The smoky smell in this bar brings him to mind.

He died long before you were born, Emma, and I've never talked about him much. I was twenty-six years old when he died at the age of ninety-three. I am not in a relationship and I have no marriage prospects on the horizon. In his world, I am doomed to be an "old maid" and his parting words to me before he died reflect that attitude.

"You'll just shrivel up down there. You're good for nothing."

This is accompanied by a very dismissive Italian gesture, a flick of his thumb from teeth outward toward me. As with so many things I experience with Cé, I don't know how to respond. So I do what I do best— stay silent and pretend those words are funny. Another unpleasant memory stored in the vault of unspoken things, best left untouched.

But right now memories of Cé are out of the vault. What can I tell you about him, Emma? Even though he isn't much taller than 5' 2" he commands a large presence in our family. He is quite round in the belly and he always wears pants that are a particular shade of brown—not tan, not dark brown—I always think of them as "Ce's colour." I don't have a name for it, but I know it is ugly. He wears suspenders, and often hooks his thumbs under the suspenders to make his chest look bigger. That gesture always reminds me of a rooster getting ready to crow, puffing out his chest and taking up even more space. He smells of cigars and wine, tomato sauce, garlic and chili peppers. He is a good cook and often makes food for our family, even when he doesn't come to our house to share in the meals with us. One of us kids is assigned to pick up what he has made.

I'm shaken out of remembering when our bottle of red house wine arrives. I don't have to know much about the finer points of wine to enjoy this moment, this experience, sharing time and space with my travelling companions. The arrival of wine is our signal to relax and share the high and low points of our day.

"This city doesn't have a very friendly vibe to it. I can't really pinpoint why, but that's what I'm feeling."

"It's kind of grotty, but that outdoor store was really good. I had such terrific service, and there was a wide selection of boots."

"The plaza outside is nice, but I'm having a hard time with all the smoking in the bar. I don't know if I'll ever get used to people smoking indoors."

"Isn't it wild, seeing a bullfight on the big screen?"

"Did you notice…," and we slip into sharing observations about the landscape, other pilgrims, what it feels like to carry our packs.

"How far should we walk tomorrow? What town should we aim for?"

"Is there a place where we can pick up lunch supplies on the trail tomorrow?"

I pull out the trusty guidebooks, handing one to Russell while I check out the other one. Rod has the map-book in front of him to review.

When our meal arrives, guidebooks and maps are set aside. We are completely in the moment, all our senses alive to the food in front of us. First course, kale and white bean soup. This has been a staple of the *Menu del Dia* so far. Our second courses are large portions. Rod has a heaping plate of pork ribs, along with French fries. Russell and I have ordered some kind of fried fish [*pescado*] accompanied by French fries as well. I'm expecting I won't like the meal because everything in the second course is fried, but I'm pleasantly surprised. This food is tasty. I only eat half of my fries, and push my plate into the centre of the table for the two men to finish off. They do, while I drift off into the Emma-zone again.

I'm missing you, Emma, someone I know I could open up to in a way that I'm not able to with the men. I try to imagine what you are doing right now, and whether you have started to make any of the changes you were talking about before we left. Have you found any courses or further education programs that interest you? Are you looking for a job? Would you consider working in a restaurant again? Are you thinking about leaving your relationship with B? I have to be honest; I've always felt like B treats you with bullying energy. I know he takes care of you and doesn't expect you to work outside the home. You've accepted his terms when you moved in together. And yet, I see that you are capable of so much more. I see you as a young woman who has been marking time, choosing to be immersed in the world of computer gaming. My misgivings about your choices continue to loom large. I lie awake at night sometimes, wondering if your time on the computer will end up eating away all your life energy, and sap your desire to move out into what I call "the real world." Will you be able to free yourself from the seductive pull of those games you play and the online friends you say are so important to you?

We've had conversations about this before, and I've heard you say, "Mom, my gaming friends are as real to me as your in-person friends. We talk to each other, we can support each other. And there's always someone who is awake and on the computer when I am. I know people in Japan, Australia, and countries in Europe."

I'm still not convinced. My anxiety about your well-being is in the red-line Worry Zone.

This is a time I have to remind myself that I found my way through a confusing start to adulthood. Maybe it will help if I let you know something about where I've come from. I've told you that I smoked pot in high school—or at least I think I've told you that. Well, that isn't the whole story. When I left home to go to university, I started using drugs more than ever. I didn't limit myself to marijuana. I wanted to try everything. So I said yes to LSD the first time it was offered to me and kept dropping acid after that. I loved being on acid trips. I used other hard drugs and occasionally, cocaine. I was binge drinking too, to the point where I would have blackouts and not remember chunks of time. I'd wake up in the morning and wonder how I got to wherever I was. I hung out with a partying crowd, mostly concerned with where the next event was going to be. I felt out of control. Whenever I was sober I felt guilty as hell, depressed, like a loser. Yet I couldn't seem to stop.

One night I seriously considered shooting up heroin. I had friends in the room who were using, women I never would have imagined would go that far. In that moment, heroin seemed enormously appealing. Thankfully, even as I considered taking up the syringe in front of me, I felt the intense presence of a white-light-being telling me that I deserved better than this. Telling me I had to stop. I listened to those words. Without saying a word, I grabbed my jacket and walked out of that dingy room. I didn't go back to that apartment, and I never spoke to those friends again. That was the beginning of weaning myself off of drugs and alcohol. I was shaken to the core on two counts: first of all, realizing that I would consider going further in my drug use, and secondly, that a protective energy showed up to stop me. What was that?

I haven't ever confided in anyone about how lost I felt, or how out of control my life was. I certainly didn't want my family to know, although I found out later they were all very worried about me. No one ever came to talk to me directly. I have felt such shame about those years, and yet now, looking back, I wouldn't change them for anything. I accept that I had to go through those hard times to get where I am today.

So I draw from my own experience, and know that you have some learning to do, in your time and in your own way. I imagine you in a few years, having learned more about yourself and what matters to you. I remember my choices as a young adult, and hold a loving space for you. I believe in you and who you are becoming. Even if you forget, I will remember a bigger version of Emma.

The negative energy of Logrono seems to be reflected in how the pilgrims in the *albergue* treat each other. Huffy, short-tempered and less respectful. There is a crowd of younger people, perhaps university age, completely disregarding the noise curfew and talking loudly in our dorm room late into the night. Even when others around them are asking for quiet.

I hear angry whispers in the dark: *"Silencio!"* "Silence!" *"Schweigen!"*

The directives are ignored.

Before I finally fall asleep, I think of Cé, and wonder if this group is from Italy.

CHAPTER 11

APRIL 26, DAY 8
LOGRONO TO VENTOSA
(20 KM)

As I leave the *albergue* this morning I am approached by a young man asking for money. "I need to make important phone calls. I've lost my cell phone."

At least that's what I understand of his story, told in broken English. I don't believe him, but he keeps moving closer into my personal space. The walls of the front courtyard surround us, and I keep stepping backwards. I don't want to be cornered, and I feel quite vulnerable. *Where are Rod and Russell?* I wonder in some fear. I reluctantly hand over a few Euros. Even though I know I am being hustled, this young man is so persistent I can't find the place inside of myself to say no. Rod and Russell finally come outside to join me, and as we start walking away, I see that young man drinking wine with friends and laughing as he points to me. This infuriates me! I tell Rod and Russell about our exchange.

Russell asks, "How come you gave him money? You should have just said no." I don't think he has any idea how hard it can be for a woman in this situation. That "just say no" business sounds so easy until confronted by a large threatening presence. This is the first time I feel like a target. Although there are beggars positioned at the entrances to the cathedrals, their presence is far less aggressive. My experience with this young man is a sharp contrast to my pilgrimage so far, so different from the high regard I feel from people I meet along the way. I am only too happy to leave Logrono behind this morning. However, the realization that I need to cover another thirty kilometres today weighs heavily on my mind. As I slog my way through the pouring rain, I feel overwhelmed by what lies ahead. More days of pushing my body through whatever the weather and trail conditions provide. I'm tired from not enough sleep last night and whatever reserves I may have had to push through adversity seem non-existent. I quietly carry on, one heavy, muddy boot in front of another, in a state of anguish about our ambitious itinerary. The changes we talked about yesterday sounded good in theory. Now, I feel such dread. Really? We're going to cover this outrageous distance every day for the next twenty-three days? Are Rod and Russell truly okay with this plan? As much as I want to be tough enough to keep walking at this pace to cover such big distances, I don't know how much longer I can do this. It's ironic, since I'm the one who cooked up the idea of walking the Camino in the first place. Russell is fit and young and gets bored quickly if he isn't in motion. I'm doing my best to make sure that I'm keeping up my end, not wanting to let him down. At the same time, continuing at this pace feels like I'm doing self-harm.

I have enough experience with self-harm, I grumble to myself. Memories of an earlier time have been insistent, demanding a front-row seat in my consciousness.

*　*　*

We have just moved to Vancouver Island and I am in our new home, feeling as if I have no roots, no connections, no support for this time of huge transition. I have no paid work, and no motivation to look for a job. Russell and Emma are not living at home any more. My body is going through menopause and my interest in life is swirling clockwise down a dark hole. I feel as if I have no reason to live anymore and I can feel my senses shutting down. I don't know how to reach out. I don't know anyone in this new community well enough to confide in. I retreat deeper into silence every day.

"How could anyone ever understand what I'm feeling right now? I don't know how to put this into words."

My depression hit its lowest point during our first summer on Vancouver Island, while Rod is doing summer archaeology fieldwork that takes him away for weeks at a time. I start believing that I'm toxic, that the world will be better off without me. When Rod is home I do my best to appear functional and alive. I take the time to make simple meals. By this time I'm eating nothing but salads. He does his best to support me since it's impossible to avoid noticing my emotional difficulties. I don't create many openings for discussion. When he asks, "What's going on?" I say very little. "I'm okay. I just feel quiet today."

He tries making helpful suggestions, encouraging me to be checked out by my family doctor. I even go so far as making an appointment. My doctor writes out a prescription which I never fill. As much as I'm suffering, I can't bring myself to start taking medication.

Rod and I don't have much ability to communicate with each other about this level of pain. When he goes away for more fieldwork I retreat deeper into my silent suffering. If the phone rings, I don't answer it. When I hear the doorbell, I stay upstairs, hardly breathing, waiting for the person on the other side to go away.

I spend endless hours wondering, *How can I kill myself?*

I consider options, with one rule: My death must look like an accident.

I do not want to cause additional pain to my family members by having them know I have committed suicide. Every day is an agony of having to carry on when the endless looping tape goes on in my head, snippets of which sound like this:

What is the point of staying here? If I'm dead, would anyone even notice? The world would be a better place if I wasn't here.

Is this the day I end it? There's a bus. I could step in front of it. Or maybe that fast-moving car.

What are the ways that suicide can look like an accident? I could drive off the edge of this bridge and into that ravine.

I hold on to needing my suicide to look like an accident. Several weeks into agonizing thoughts about how I can "accidentally" end my life, I come up with the idea of using food to kill myself after a friend of mine is hospitalized for an intestinal blockage and nearly dies. I wonder if grapes will do the job. I buy a bunch of the Red Globe variety, thinking that if I try to swallow one whole that will put an end to me. I am strangely excited to begin this experiment, looking forward to the end of my meaningless pain. I take that first grape, pop it into my mouth and swallow it. It goes down without lodging anywhere! How can that be? That's not supposed to happen. I try again. Same thing. I swallow three more whole grapes, thinking that if I don't choke on them, their large size is going to cause some blockage in my digestive system, somewhere. I am amazed at the size of food bits I can swallow without choking.

After twenty-four hours, nothing has changed. No pain, no discomfort, no indication that anything is going awry. I need to come up with another plan. It's cherry season, and I do love B.C. cherries. So my next trial is to swallow the cherry pits rather than spit them out. Over a period of three days I consume at least a pound of cherries and swallow every pit. After that time, my digestive tract is still in working order, and I'm no closer to death. *I must have quite the constitution,* I think to myself.

My final attempt at blocking up my system is with apples. I decide to try eating the seeds and cores of every apple I consume. I feel more like a horse, or a four-legged creature of the world. Certainly not very civilized. And no matter what I've done so far, my digestion is fine, I experience minimal physical discomfort. And yet the days continue in endless emotional pain. I am desperate to have my suffering come to an end. I have occasional breaks from this internal agony, when I agree to go for a walk in the forest with a friend. These walks are the only times that I feel any sense of relief. I keep conversations on the surface, friendly as I can possibly be, making sure that I'm asking the questions.

"Have you had any visitors lately?"

"Do you have any plans for travel in the next while?"

"What are some good groups to volunteer with here in the valley?"

I deflect attention away from myself.

When I return home, I wonder, *How long will it take me to die if I don't drink any water or eat any food?* I know that dying from starvation takes about forty days. I have already fasted for ten days at a stretch, so why not try for longer?

Living without water will be a quicker end than going without food.

I try and find I can't ignore thirst as long as water is available. I don't drink much, but those sips I am taking keep me alive. My skin is wrinkling from dehydration, yet I am still alive.

As I deprive myself of food and water over many days, my life is reduced to reading stacks of romance novels from the library; I don't leave the house much and I continue avoiding the phone or answering the door. I shrink away from human contact as my body is shrivelling away. At one point I weigh less than ninety-five pounds. I am proud that I am finally thin enough. Even I can see that I have no body fat but my sense of self does not improve. After many weeks of near starvation I have an epiphany moment riding a B.C. ferry back to Vancouver Island after dropping Rod on the mainland for more fieldwork. My body takes over from my brain, *Eat! Now!*

I head over to the Coastal Café where I order a chicken salad wrap. I go back for yam fries. Then a banana. This is my turning point; over time my suicidal thoughts slowly recede without any outside intervention. My will to live continues to strengthen as I slowly re-engage with people I love, and activities I truly enjoy.

*   *   *

My fifteen weeks of frozen silence remain unspoken about between Rod and me. Whatever thoughts he has about that time have never been discussed. Yet I suspect they are festering away, needing to be acknowledged in some way. The trail seems endless to me this morning, as I walk the gravel path alongside fields of tender green shoots that may be a grain, maybe a feed crop for animals. A grey overcast sky and barren tree branches in the distance match how I feel inside.

My encounter with the young man at the *refugio* this morning shook me up so much I have pulled completely into myself. *Just leave me alone*, my body language screams. I feel overwhelmed by the volume of travellers on the road now. I walk the first few hours without greeting other pilgrims. I don't want to acknowledge anyone's presence as they pass by. Yet it is impossible to escape the onslaught of others, especially as they cheerily call out, "*Buen Camino!*" or "*Hola peregrinos!*" as they breeze by me. It's going to be a very long day.

When I start to feel hungry enough for lunch I announce, "This looks like a good spot for a break." But for Rod, that's his signal to start looking for a better place to sit down. He keeps walking, as if I haven't said a thing. I feel my insides unravelling. In my mind I am shouting, *I need to stop now!* I imagine screaming at the top of my lungs: *I'm not going to walk another hour just so you can find the goddam perfect spot. I'm tired, I'm hungry, and my feet are in fucking spasms. You go ahead. I'm stopping here! Just go ahead. I'm done! I am so ready to do the rest of this Camino alone.*

I fume along in silence, falling behind Rod and Russell, my pouting lower lip getting lower to the ground. I understand more deeply how Emma must have felt, trailing behind us, wishing we would stop. My mind goes around in hamster-wheel circles: *Why do I have to work so hard to convince Rod that I need to stop? It really doesn't matter to me how perfect the spot is right now!*

I'm so weary of having to rationalize anything I need or want. I am sick of hearing Rod say "No" to every idea I have. When I declare I'm going to mail extra equipment on to myself in Santiago, I hear Rod say, "No, you shouldn't do that. It might not get there."

When I am looking for an automated bank teller to take out cash, I hear Rod's voice saying, "No, this isn't the right ATM machine to take out your money."

I hear Rod say "No" to taking breaks at times that suit me. I want to stomp my feet like a two-year-old.

As a mother of two young children, I didn't like hearing "No." Just before Russell turned two, he started using that word. When he screamed at me with his little face enraged, "NO!" I wanted to smack him! *I'm bigger than you, damn it. Why don't you just do what I say?* My guts tightened in a knot and my jaw clenched; everything in me fought the impulse to use physical punishment as a way to get him to do what I wanted. Options ran through my head: a good swift kick to the butt; yelling louder and calling him names; walking away and just leaving him there; banishing him to a room by himself. Then I heard Kitty's calm and patient voice in my head, the woman teaching my parenting classes: *Just remember that when he's a teenager, you're going to want him to say no. Start now.*

Russell has moved well beyond the "No" phase, unlike his father who continues to respond with his automatic no before considering other options. I'm back to wondering,

Why do I have to justify every freaking impulse I have?
Isn't it enough just to want something? I feel like I have
to run through the male analytical filters every time I say
something. I'm calling it the "slice and dice" approach to
conversation. I'm worn down to the point where I don't
want to say anything. I am that tired. I turn to my daughter:

Emma, this might be too much information, but Rod
is clearly letting me know that he doesn't have much
time for my thoughts and impressions. I hear statements
like, "You've already said that!" Especially if it has
to do with reflections on my upbringing, anything to
do with memories of my mother, or how I'm piecing
things together now. Like what I shared earlier with
you about Cé. He wouldn't give me the time of day
about any of those memories, yet that's what is
surfacing so strongly each day. I wish I could put a
cork in this brain of mine and stop the remembering.
Sometimes I'm hungry for conversation that isn't
just about facts and physical information but I can't
think of anything to open up a communication line. I
censor myself because I can't bear what I expect to
hear.

"You've said that already."

"That's so negative."

"Can't you just enjoy where you are right now?"

"Buddhists teach about being in the moment."

Comments like these are thrown out like judgments,
at a time when I feel so present to my surroundings I
can hardly bear it. It's a strange paradox—the more
in the moment I feel, the more my body releases
these memories. The gap between Rod and me seems

to be widening. I feel like he uses his knowledge of Buddhist teachings and meditation as a weapon. At the same time, I am not experiencing his energy as embodying presence and mindfulness, so how does he get to be the expert?

In the midst of my internal anguish, I plod along behind the guys. Russell keeps checking on me, looking over his shoulder. He finally intervenes, saying, "This looks like a good place to stop." Now Rod listens. When we finally sit down for lunch and I look down at the slice of bread I am cutting for my sandwich, I burst into tears. Unexpectedly. Intensely. Trying to cry quietly. When Rod and Russell look up at me to hand me the cheese and salami, they both seem startled by my wet face. It's no longer raining.

Russell asks, "What's wrong?"

Between sobs, I tell him: "I can't eat another piece of bread! My body aches. I don't WANT to walk thirty kilometres today. I can't keep pushing like this all the way to Santiago. There's no time to slow down and enjoy where we are. I wonder what the hell I'm doing here!"

There's an awkward silence, the two men looking at each other, baffled and confused, not sure how to respond. I keep my head down, uncertain what I'll hear next. Russell is the first to speak.

"I came because I am kind of in a rut at work. I'm hoping I'll come away from this time with some answers. Plus I wanted an adventure. None of my friends had the interest or the money to go on a trip like this. I like the walking, but I'm frustrated that we have to move so slowly. I could keep going at these distances every day."

Rod says, "I'm enjoying myself, mostly. I'm interested in the history and the architecture along this route. The trail is varied, and I like the colours of the landscape. I'm actually relieved that you said something about cutting back on our daily distances."

So I have more support than I expected in Rod. Thankfully, Russell is willing to adjust our plans if that's what is needed to keep going as a team.

I return to my now-soggy bread and finish making my sandwich. I have mixed feelings. Resenting that it takes my breaking down in tears before Rod chooses to listen. This isn't the first time. One particular episode stands out in this moment. After Russell was born, it was many long weeks before Rod touched me in an intimate way. I felt so lonely for his caress and love, yet he would pull away from me at night when I reached out for him. When I let out my feelings in a teary night-time outburst, he finally disclosed that all the changes to my body since I had our baby were difficult for him to adjust to. It took that painful conversation for intimacy to finally return.

Mixed in with resentment is my relief that we've decided to change our itinerary. My whole body relaxes knowing we are cutting out some distance from today's walk. While Rod takes a nap, Russell and I spend our remaining break time reading through the guidebooks to see how far we should travel today.

Russell suggests, "Instead of stopping in Najera tonight let's stop in Ventosa."

I ask, "How far is that from here?"

He does a quick check, then tells me, "Well, looking at the map and reading what's in here, probably another ten kilometres. Can you do that?" I breathe a huge sigh of relief. "Yes, that's very doable. Thank you!"

As we resume walking at our adjusted pace, I find that I can listen more fully to the Spanish-speaking birds, take more time with the flowers, and hear what the land has to say. I have more time to let myself experience the wonder, the pain, the openings in my body. More space for silence to weave its magic inside of me.

After supper, Russell and I sit together to refine our itinerary, working backwards from Finisterre. We're calling our new plan "Camino 2.0." Reducing our walking distance each day means that we need to find a way to make up the kilometres we aren't covering, either by taking more time to complete our Camino (not possible due to our son's desire to participate in an event in Barcelona after our walk), or taking a bus from one city to another. Camino 2.0 cuts out the walking between Burgos and Ponferrada, the region known as the *Meseta*. We plan to take the bus from Burgos to León, then from León to Ponferrada. We'll be walking over 650 kilometres, finishing at Finisterre rather than ending our walk at Santiago de Compostela.

Even though we've all agreed to change our plans, I wonder if I will finish this walk by myself, or if the three of us will stay together. I'm on the fence about the state of my relationship with Rod. We could enter Santiago together and still part ways afterwards.

CHAPTER 12

APRIL 27, DAY 9
VENTOSA TO AZOFRA
(16 KM)

This morning the weather mirrors my mood; sun is shining, it's not too warm, perfect for walking. I feel like a great weight has been lifted from my shoulders. Russell seems to have picked up some kind of bug. It's zapped his energy even though he's still able to walk. He needs many bathroom breaks. Rod's talking about how his back and blisters are bothering him, too, and maybe he's letting me know about his aches and pains now that we have a less ambitious schedule. How much were we all silencing ourselves in our commitment to the group goal?

There are other reasons for the change in my mood. My pack is lighter now. We hiked the nine kilometres into Najera yesterday and found the *Oficina de Correros* where I mailed my excess gear to Santiago. We were obviously not the first ones to do so. The post office had good quality cardboard boxes of all shapes and sizes to contain gear, packing tape, and prepared labels addressed to the Santiago post office nearest the Cathedral. I was also able to speak English with one of the employees, which made a potentially difficult transaction very easy.

I got rid of my long underwear, my nightie—I can sleep in my clean shirt—a book, a compression stuff sack and my photo download kit, not useable at Internet cafes. The total weight of what the three of us collectively sent ahead was five kilograms, with most of it from Russell and me. I notice the difference in the weight of my pack immediately as I stepped out of the post office and back onto the trail. I am puzzled by Rod's attachment to the heavy weight he's carrying. Even after Russell and I pointed out items we thought he didn't need to carry anymore, they all stayed in his pack. Maybe he doesn't trust the Spanish postal service. Is it that hard for him to let go? Perhaps he has something to prove to himself about being a man, or how aging hasn't affected his abilities. I've seen this quality in him before, where he has a goal in mind, then persists in spite of his hard work that yields little or no results. I recall the way Rod keeps working away in our Calgary backyard, turning compost every week, trying to get our garden vegetables to grow, even though the soil is heavy clay. There is an old tree stump in the middle of the garden space. Several large trees in our backyard take up most of the available nutrients and keep the sunlight away from the garden plants. I keep saying, "Give it up. If we're ever going to have a garden that produces anything, we need to invest money, change the location and get some topsoil." But we don't have the extra money, so every year, Rod works diligently, adding vegetable matter to the compost pile and turning it. Preparing the garden bed in the spring, digging up the soil and breaking the hard ground, sometimes with a mattock because it's so hard. Starting some seedlings to transplant; directly seeding others. And then watching the disappointing results as plants don't germinate, or they sprout and wither, or they grow and don't produce anything at all. Every summer we harvest tiny carrots that are almost too small to eat.

Perhaps it's hard for Rod to change course. However, today is a day of celebration. I suggest, "Let's not have another bread-meat-cheese lunch on the trail." Rod quickly agrees. "Great idea." We head over to the nearest bar that is serving food when we're feeling ready for lunch. We enjoy a full meal in a small restaurant filled with locals and some pilgrims. We sit next to Heinrich from Germany, who tells us all about the walkers he has gotten to know so far.

"Have you met Ingrid? She's a university student who's taking a year off to travel."

"I've been meeting up with Johann at night, he's become a very good friend. He's from the Netherlands. We have a lot in common and we like the same kinds of wine."

"I can't walk very fast because my hips and knees bother me. I'm taking a long time to do my Camino. My wife has no interest in this kind of activity, so here I am, on my own."

Heinrich manages to consume an entire bottle of wine by himself.

"This is lunch time," I whisper to Rod and Russell. "How can he walk after drinking all that alcohol?"

We often leave a small amount of wine in our bottle at the end of a meal. But not today, not for this celebration. It is a shorter walking day, after all.

We must be getting acculturated to Spain, because after our lunch and a short time walking, Rod declares he needs a break. Maybe the wine is having an effect. While he is having his *siesta*, I take time to write in my journal. Russell pulls out his sketchbook and plays with line drawings. Spending our time like this was not possible before, but now with reduced distances between stages, we can follow the natural rhythms of our bodies.

The one person who may not be totally happy with our itinerary change is Russell. His younger body is capable of so much more, and I know we're holding him back. Yet, whenever I suggest that he could go ahead, and we meet up with him somewhere further along the trail, he hangs with us. At the same time I continue to notice some tension between Rod and Russell. Rod is a man who is most at ease with dispensing information. When our kids were younger, it was easy for their father to be the one they looked up to, with so many facts at his fingertips. Rod, Russell and Emma would sit around the table for hours after a meal, discussing how things work, why dinosaurs no longer walk the earth, how long it took for a national railway to be built across Canada. I would typically lose interest and wander off to read a book or do some writing.

Russell is an adult now, and he's no longer so willing to be the receptacle of Rod's knowledge. In fact, Russell has his own well-developed interests and the courses he studied at university have given him a new framework for looking at the world around us. This is evident in the conversations we have while walking. I'm getting an art history education from my son as he describes theories of art and the role of art in culture. I openly admit I know nothing about these topics, so I'm like a sponge. There's a difference in the way I listen to Russell and how I respond to Rod. I'm more curious to hear what Russell talks about. Is it because he's more attentive to me on the trail? Am I so closed off to Rod I don't want to listen to what he has to say, no matter what it is?

There are times when I feel like I'm on the verge of being drawn into an argument between the two men, where I might end up being asked to take sides. I do my best to stay well out of the way, holding back my opinions. It takes mental energy for me to find a way of listening to facts and physical observations about our surroundings. I suspect that's a male way of experiencing the world, which is much different than the dream-like mental space I occupy these days. I'm not so concerned about hard facts. I don't need to know details about the structures and landscape around me. If I don't know a name for something, I make it up. My brain comes up with outlandish possibilities for why things are the way they are, and I am loving this opportunity to let my imagination roam without constraint.

As we resume walking after Rod's *siesta*, I am more fully awake to my surroundings. The red hillsides remind me of the Red Deer River badlands that we travelled through by canoe. Rough rounded shapes, cut by a river that has dried up after spring run-off, the pathway of the water visible from a distance. The vineyards continue to have a presence along this route; we have lost the olive groves. I marvel at the snow-capped mountains in the distance. Old aqueducts are visible in the fields; some look functional while others have grass growing in them.

We are now travelling with a familiar crowd of people that we have been getting to know in the *refugios* and on the trail. At each encounter we learn more about who they are, where they come from, what motivated their walk on the Camino. We leapfrog each other during the day, shouting out friendly greetings or walking along together in a companionable conversation. I speak with a woman from Finland who is a marathon runner; she doesn't stay long with us. Felix is a young German man who seems very impulsive, wandering off in wrong directions. Although he walks quickly, he doesn't often make the right choices at intersections. We keep meeting up with him as he returns to the correct route. We laugh to ourselves, thinking he's probably walking twice the regular distance.

"I never thought I would need to speak German in Spain," comments Rod. It's true. There are a surprising number of German pilgrims, in addition to people from many other countries. The Camino is a snapshot of people from countries all over the world. I had no idea this pilgrim route is so well-known, or so well-travelled, even in the spring. I am not able to speak with some walkers, like pilgrims from Brazil who only speak Portuguese. I keep seeing a solo female hiker from Korea, walking in silence. I hear from fellow travellers that there's a group of Japanese monks on this route who are shocked at the opulence of the Camino. That statement prompts me to reflect on the quality of my Camino so far. I have been gradually allowing myself more creature comforts. I've gone from thinking I have to push my body hard all the way to Santiago to cutting back on daily distances. We're going to take a bus to help make up the distance we can't cover. If we don't like the look of a pilgrim hostel, we stay in private accommodation. I do my best to enjoy my meals rather than feeling guilty although I'm still not comfortable with how much I'm eating. I hear Valentine's voice in my head asking questions like: *Are you sure you want to eat that second piece of bread?* Or my own voice: *I wish I hadn't put so much on my plate for breakfast this morning.* This journey seems to be about being kinder to myself, learning to lighten my load, and deciding what I will pick up again once I've arrived home.

For supper we have a very light meal with the fruit and cheese we're carrying. I love the simplicity of the food we eat tonight. It's a relief to eat a small amount for a change. And I get the added bonus of extra moments for reading and solitude.

Tomorrow we plan to stop in Grañón, where one of the *refugios* is maintained and staffed with volunteer *hospitaleros* from all over the world. The Canadian Company of Pilgrims typically provides volunteers for four weeks each year. I've heard so much about this spot, it's built up to almost mythic proportions in my mind.

CHAPTER 13

APRIL 28, DAY 10
AZOFRA TO GRAÑÓN
(23 KM)

My walking today is inspired by my vision of staying at the *refugio* in Grañón. When I attended the Victoria Pilgrim Gathering in March, I learned that the Canadian Company of Pilgrims offers training and support for *hospitaleros*, and Grañón is one of the postings for Canadian volunteers. Ever since that pilgrim gathering, I made a commitment to make sure we stop here on our journey. I have heard nothing but glowing descriptions from all the pilgrims I talked to before we left Canada.

"It's so special."

"I think Grañón was the highlight for me."

"You have to stay there!"

I understand that the places to sleep are inside the bell tower of the parish church, so I begin constructing that image in my mind. Our Confraternity of Saint James guidebook tells us the *refugio* is *donativo*, that there is a communal supper AND breakfast served by the *hospitaleros*. This sounds generous to me, and I'm feeling ready to receive, unlike earlier times in my life when I felt undeserving of kindness. I recall growing up in the Catholic faith, taught that I was born with original sin. I took that to heart, and when I was old enough to think about such things, I wondered how black my soul was, each sin I committed darkening that white soul a little more. I'd go to confession, which cleansed my soul—apparently—and then the blackening process would begin all over again.

*   *   *

I believe I am tainted with some inner flaw, since I feel so harshly judged by God. At the same time, I love the rituals of the Catholic High Mass, and look forward to the special Church celebrations like Easter and Christmas. There's some sense of magic in the Latin incantations, the songs, the incense, the sacred ceremony in which I am an observer, not a participant.

As a child and teenager, I am expected to memorize and speak prayers aloud in school religion classes and at home. I recite many rosaries—often on my knees—at my mother's insistence. Fingers moving through the sequence of beads, saying aloud, "Hail Mary, full of grace, the Lord is with thee. Blessed art thou amongst women and blessed is the fruit of thy womb, Jesus," followed by one, "I believe in the Father, the Son and the Holy Ghost. As it was in the beginning is now and ever shall be, world without end, Amen." I learn all the proper responses for the Sacraments of First Communion and Confirmation. However even though I memorize many prayers, regurgitating memorized passages at designated moments doesn't feel like a conversation with God.

*   *   *

I seem to know more about what prayer isn't, rather than what it is. Deep inside I feel a sense of longing for a sense of spiritual connection that eludes me. I've been asking questions regarding religion, power, spirituality, and connection to the Divine, all the way to right here, right now. That's another reason I'm anxious to get to the *refugio* in Grañón. I've read that evening prayers are sung in the church and I'm intrigued. I've yet to attend any of the pilgrim services after we finish our day of walking, and I feel a desire to experience at least one. Staying within the church could remove the excuses I seem so able to come up with, especially since Rod and Russell aren't interested. At least up until now they haven't been, and without them joining me, I lose momentum when the time for an evening pilgrim mass draws near. I'm confused by the push-pull of my desire to attend a service; my resistance always wins out. Will Grañón be where I arrive at enlightenment?

I get so involved creating my image of what I'll find waiting for me at the end of this day, I barely pay attention to my surroundings. Unconsciously, I'm re-creating one the towers from my fantasy play as a child. Each step I take results in another elaborate addition to this imaginary structure. Tapestries are hanging from the walls. Stained glass windows colour the light coming into the building. Hand-hewn wood furniture, well-loved and cared for, is placed artfully throughout the pilgrim accommodation. It's like when I'd go into the confessional after I'd received my first communion, and imagine that behind a secret door was a set of stairs that would take me into a special room that no one else but me could find. And that room was full of gemstones, gold and soft light from candles, soft hand-woven rugs on the floor and warmth emanating from a fireplace.

When we finally arrive, the tower sleeping area is full. Two *hospitaleros* are busily laying out sleeping mats on the main floor of the building, the overflow section for all the extra bodies that will be staying overnight. Mats are apparently the standard sleeping arrangement here, not bunk beds. We take one look at the number of people crowding in at the entrance, the thin mats lying side-by-side in the dusty, musty stone overflow room, and quickly decide to look for an alternative place to stay. My mood plummets, and I'm not alone in my disappointment. We feel so let down after the build-up. Still, we have to find shelter and food for the night no matter our reactions.

Through patient, slow questioning in Spanish, Rod finds us a pension in the small town. The room is clean and comfortable, part of a large house that's been renovated to accommodate pilgrims, with a locked door, three single beds, and its own bathroom. This kind of privacy is in short supply in the *refugios*. We're comfortable sharing the same sleeping space on this journey, probably because it's not much different than sharing a tent as we have done on many family camping trips. I'm aware this also means Rod and I are keeping our physical distance.

We each take some quiet time for ourselves, relishing this space. Rod naps, Russell reads, and I write in my journal. My words record the surprise I feel as I recognize how quickly I let go of my expectations, choosing not to hang on to my disappointment. Is this the magic of the Camino?

When my hunger starts to kick in, I declare, "Time to find a place to eat." I get no argument from the two men.

Instead of sharing our supper in a large group at the *refugio*, we find a small bar where the woman who runs the place seems thrilled to pieces to be able to serve us a pilgrim meal. My mood lifts as I bask in her attention. Even when I confuse her by ordering coffee before my meal will arrive, she beams at me. She asks twice, trying to make sure she has heard me correctly. Then she goes off to make coffee with a wide smile on her face. As I look at her retreating back, I suddenly recall that in Spain coffee is served *after* the meal. No wonder she asked twice; it wasn't just my poor language skills. What other cultural transgressions have I been making along the way? I marvel at all the different cultures represented on this journey so far and how much adjustment is required by everyone, travellers and locals alike. Somehow, in a way I don't fully understand, the Camino is a great equalizer. It's as if we've all made unspoken agreements to begin the long walk, and those who support us have also made choices to offer us what they can, with a measure of grace and respect. It doesn't always happen, but so far, more often than not. The service I am receiving tonight highlights the respect I have felt as a pilgrim on this route.

When I take the time to look around, I observe that we are almost the only patrons in the bar at this early hour—it's not even close to supper hour for the locals—and my sense of loneliness and isolation returns. No other pilgrims are in sight. Is it unusual for pilgrims to frequent the local establishments? The *hospitaleros* in the Grañón *refugio* must be run off their feet, taking care of all the arrivals today, including preparing and serving a meal. My mind drifts off into a grey zone, a rather numb state between thought and no thought, my eyes staring off at nothing. Then our first course of kale and bean soup arrives, delivered by the same woman who took our orders. She beams at us like a beacon of love. I shift from feeling lonely and disappointed to taking in the warmth of her expression. Even though I can barely carry on a conversation with her, I feel her radiating a sense of, *I'm so glad you're here.*

My gloominess melts away once again.

Not only that, it's hard to stay gloomy in front of a plate of food when I'm hungry. As I slowly savour my white bean soup with greens, my spirit lifts another notch or two. I take the time to inhale the rich scent of broth, seasoned with thyme, oregano, and basil. Then my main course, featuring roasted chicken, is brought out, and I'm excited again to have something different from the usual *Menu del Dia.* The dessert is a flan, a dish we've had often on this trip, but tonight I find it especially enjoyable. It might just be the love that this food has been prepared with that makes it all seem so delicious.

As I saunter back to our pension for the night, I am full in every way from the service we have received. The outpouring of love and attention from a woman with whom I can barely carry on a conversation has been my warm welcome. I didn't read about this in any of my guidebooks

CHAPTER 14

APRIL 29, DAY 11
GRAÑÓN TO VILLAMBISTIA
(22.5 KM)

The weather starts out windy and overcast, not very warm. It is one of those days where I just want to put my head down and walk, intent on covering the miles. It doesn't help my enjoyment level to spend most of the day walking beside a very busy highway. In fact, I feel like we could be walking between Calgary and Banff. When I voice this thought out loud, Russell comments, "Walking to Banff would be more scenic." I couldn't agree more. Adding to the sense of misery I'm feeling are my foot cramps. Once again, they have started up after about two or three hours of walking. I choose to feel the pain without saying anything more about it, rather than bother Rod and Russell with more complaints. My feet release their memories.

* * *

We have just moved into our new house. I am no more than eight years old. A family friend is visiting Valentine in our shiny new living room with its shiny new furniture. My younger brother and I are running around and I slice my foot open on a curtain rod left lying on the floor. My foot is bleeding a lot and my brother keeps insisting that I show Mom. I refuse. She has company in the living room. She hates to be interrupted when there are visitors. She gets so mad when I'm hurt, especially when there's blood involved. So I do my best to take care of everything myself. I swear my brother to silence too.

*   *   *

My Camino flashback is interrupted in an unexpected way. We arrive at a *baño* stop where there is a gathering of people using the bathrooms provided by a gas station along the highway. While waiting in the lineup for my turn, I strike up conversations with other women. I feel an immediate kinship with my fellow female walkers. I break through my usual barriers of reserve by speaking with an Australian woman in front of me.

Me: "Where are you headed today?"

She: "I'm not sure. I just walk until I feel myself getting tired. Then I start looking for a place to stay."

Me: "What a great way to travel. That's even more unstructured than we are. Do you have a certain number of days to travel?"

She: "I've given myself seven weeks to get to Santiago. I don't want to push myself, so I'm taking my time and letting my body tell me how far to go. I've never done anything like this before. I'm not in the best shape."

Me: "I love how you're travelling. We have an idea of where we want to go each day, and we are somewhat flexible. But we're still trying to cover at least twenty kilometres a day. I think it takes courage to be so open with your schedule."

She: "Well I'm impressed at how far you are able to walk each day. I could never do that."

I bask in her feedback. It's a welcome drop of nourishment in a sometimes barren field of acknowledgment. Not only is it comforting to speak, in English, with another woman, I am pleasantly surprised that she is impressed I am walking at a faster pace than she is. Over the past couple of days I've been berating myself for being so slow and needing to ask Rod and Russell to slow down and cover less distance, to the point where we need to take a bus at some point to make up the lost ground.

Still waiting my turn to use the bathroom, a woman from Montreal tells me she's been wanting to meet me ever since she met Russell at the pilgrim dinner in Roncesvalles.

She: "So you are Russell's mother. I am so touched that you are walking with your son. He is such a lovely young man. Are you walking with anyone else from your family?"

Me: "Yes, my husband. It's just the three of us. We invited our daughter to come along, but she didn't think she was up for such a long walk. I miss her, but I'm really glad that I'm here. Are you travelling with anyone else?"

She: "No, I'm on my own. My husband died recently, and I'm not sure what my next life choices will be. So I've quit my job and I'm doing this walk. I'm waiting for inspiration, and I know that I will have answers by the time I reach Santiago."

This Montreal pilgrim is not the only one walking after a big life transition. We've met young people from a number of European countries who have just completed university degrees and can't find work. We hear from a young German man, "I just graduated, but the economy isn't doing all that well and jobs are hard to find, so why not go for a long walk on the Camino instead?" A young woman from the Netherlands disclosed, "I've just been laid off, so I decided I'd walk the Camino first, before trying to find another job. I'm not sure what I want to do next or where I'll want to be. I just walked out my door with my pack on my back and here I am." I'm somewhat envious that this is an option available to people here in Europe. In Canada we have nothing like this Camino network of trails.

The Confraternity of Saint James guidebook we carry with us leads us to a new *albergue* in Villambistia that sleeps fourteen people. It's run by two Brazilian men who provide a very welcoming space, including a bar and a pilgrim meal. The owners have created an inviting courtyard in which I end up spending time once I've taken care of my immediate needs. We're not sure if this place serves breakfast, but we're close to other towns that have pilgrim services so it's not a concern tonight. However, we have to wait until eight to eat, which is unfortunate, as I am hungry for supper by six o'clock.

Tonight I wish I didn't have to eat. I'm feeling tired and worn out as I reflect on how life at home would be so much simpler without having to dream up menus, buy groceries, prepare meals, serve and clean up afterwards. Sometimes just the act of eating a meal feels like too much, when my desire to avoid gaining weight kills the pleasure of trying new food, or enjoying every dish that is offered. Is this another way that I reject nourishment? Is controlling my food intake a way that I can maintain some power and control when everything else feels chaotic?

Before we eat, each pilgrim undergoes a Brazilian initiation. One of the *hospitaleros* holds a wineskin above my mouth, and releases a thin stream of wine which I am supposed to catch, like liquid popcorn. I'm pleased at my success. There was no option to decline. Had there been a choice, I would have refused. No pressure here. Raucous cheering and clapping greets the final person in the circle, and platters of roasted meat and vegetables are brought out for us to enjoy. I dig into this feast. Surprisingly, I feel quite at ease here.

We have two more days to walk in to Burgos, where we plan to stay at one of the pilgrim hostels in the centre of the city for two nights. Then we'll travel on to León by bus, stay overnight there before boarding a bus one more time to get to Ponferrada. From there we'll resume walking to Santiago and on to Finisterre. We have searched online for bus schedules so we know what time we need to be at the Burgos bus depot to leave for León.

Because we've spent so much time researching bus services and pinning down the date we need to arrive in Barcelona, we've also decided to book our place to stay in Barcelona. Doing the necessary searches and making our bookings in Internet cafes was challenging, but it's done now. This is the extent of our planning ahead. It's so much simpler to just get up in the morning and walk, following our pilgrim routines.

CHAPTER 15

APRIL 30, DAY 12
VILLAMBISTIA TO OLMOS DE ATAPUERCA
(26 KM)

My morning vision of pilgrim equanimity and ease on
the trail has quickly vanished under an onslaught of cold
wind and rain. A foreshadowing of the angry outbursts
to come.

The first one in our party to lose his cool is Rod. He has
a silent meltdown in the village of Espinosa del Camino,
where we have been planning to stop in the *café/panaderia*
indicated in our guidebook. It turns out to be a truck stop,
with the stench of diesel fuel, oil, and garbage strewn around
its rough edges. A mangy undernourished dog cowers as
we approach, but doesn't stop nosing the garbage for things
to eat. It's not up to the standard of our usual stopping
places. Still, this is where we planned to have our break and
I'm ready to stop. However, Rod refuses to go in. He doesn't
speak. Instead he just keeps on walking without telling
Russell and me what he is thinking.

Russell and I are shaken, shouting out, "You can't just
walk away!"

Rod responds in a very loud voice, "Yes I can, I'm
doing it right now."

Like an afterthought thrown over his shoulder, he
adds, "There are a lot of trucks there and I don't want
Russell to get sick."

It takes a while for Rod to slow down his pace so
that we can catch up. I feel sick to my stomach at what's

taking place, not sure what, if any, resolution there will be. Sadly, this exchange reminds me of trips with Mike and Valentine when I was a child.

* * *

Our family typically goes on two- or three-week long holidays during the summer. Dad loves driving long distances, which inevitably leads to a big blow out between Mom and Dad, a week or ten days into the journey. I can predict that after they fight my mother won't talk for the rest of the trip. One of the more memorable incidents occurs at Niagara Falls – known as The Honeymoon Capital of the World - when I am thirteen or fourteen years old. We are driving around the tourist-packed streets when Mom insists she's had enough—I don't know what the prompt is—and tries to jump out of the car while it is still moving.

We're screaming at her, "Mom, don't jump!" When Dad slows down for a red light she opens the door, leaps out, then disappears. We are silenced by fear as Dad drives around trying to find her. No luck. So he takes us to our motel, getting us settled in before he heads back out on his own. My guts are in a knot. We four siblings wait for a very long time with no sign of any parent. Dad arrives with a family-size bucket of Kentucky Fried Chicken for our supper; still no Mom. None of us have much of an appetite. Dad leaves again, continuing his search. Finally late in the evening they both return. Mom seems deflated somehow. For the remainder of the trip she maintains a stony statue presence. She doesn't participate in any decision making. She seems frozen. The rest of us carry on, trying to engage her in our surroundings, doing our best to include her and acknowledge her, with little success. Finally I decide to enjoy myself the best I can, whether she is participating or not. It's just too painful to wait for her to show any interest in us or her surroundings.

*   *   *

I try to remind myself that this Camino walk is different from my childhood vacations. In spite of our difficulties, Rod, Russell, and I have the ability to talk things over. Once we regroup and begin to calm down, the men begin to talk. I'm still caught up in my memories, so I hold back, surrounding myself in a protective silence. Russell speaks quite openly to his father, in a way I've never heard before, his temper ignited by Rod's statement, "I don't want Russell to get sick."

He challenges Rod, "That's bullshit! YOU don't want to get sick. Stop using me as your excuse to do what you want to do. It's hard for me when you're so obviously not telling the truth."

Rod finally acknowledges, "I didn't want to stop there because it was so grotty. The smell of the diesel was making me sick, and I just couldn't imagine trying to eat anything there."

During this journey I've been learning that Rod has a superior sense of smell, and I don't. I can no longer assume that if a certain odor doesn't bother me, it won't bother him. If I admit the truth about my own reactions, I didn't find the truck stop very inviting as a place to have a coffee or a snack. I just want to stop and have a break, since my feet are bothering me so much. I've been doing my best to avoid focusing on the pain of foot cramps, and I prefer not to talk about it. Instead I attend to other sensory details, or conjure up lists of what I am loving about being on the trail. However, any time I anticipate an opportunity to sit down, I look forward to it. At the end of Rod and Russell's debriefing they arrive at some measure of peace. I suspect that their relationship has shifted as a result. I see Russell establishing his place as an equal beside his father, not as the son who needs constant protection and guidance.

I'm not sure if anything much has shifted between Rod and me since we've been on the trail. We seem to be in some kind of an unspoken struggle. I'm still trying to break out of the roles I've accepted for so long, the ones that are culturally prescribed. "This is how a woman behaves. This is a wife, this is a mother, this is a daughter." I don't want to be subservient to others or be the one who nurtures everyone else without also getting something back. I want to be acknowledged for who I am. How many generations of women in my family line believed there should be no expectation of thanks or appreciation for all the work done?

Did the men ever receive words of gratitude from the women?

I've never taken the time to pay such close attention to the state of my relationship and, sadly, what shows up under the lens of examination is that Rod and I have forgotten how to show our love or appreciation for each other. I've been noticing that whenever I try to share something personal to Rod, his responses try to deflect my attention. "Look at that building." Or, "I was thinking about that design." He appears more comfortable making some comment about our physical surroundings that shuts down my impulse to say anything about my inner life. Is that part of the cultural training for men, to avoid emotional expression? Is that why, when I approach Rod to give a hug or have some physical contact, I instead receive some form of admonishment like "Watch your head," if we're near the bunk beds, or a delaying tactic like: "Wait, I have to tie my shoe/find my coat/pack my pack." Is he sick and tired of being with me? Maybe I'm not the only one who is sick and tired of being together.

These are the thoughts that occupy my mind as I resume walking. After the experience of watching Rod stomp off in a huff, where I wasn't sure what was going to happen next, or if he was even going to stop, I'm surprised by how little I could trust that he would stop and wait for me.

*   *   *

We're driving home from Edmonton with Mom at the wheel. It's winter time, snow is falling and the roads aren't in very good shape. My sister Annette, who is fourteen or so, sits in the back seat behind Mom. I'm sandwiched in the middle between Annette and one of my older brothers; my youngest brother is sitting in the front. I'm half asleep, lulled by the movement of the car. I'm jolted awake by Mom's screaming, "We're going to crash, I can't stop the car!" We're spinning in circles on the highway. My sister Annette's voice is soothing. "It's okay Mom. We'll be okay. Stay calm." She has reached over the seat to try to guide the car while mom is in panic mode. No other vehicles approach from the opposite direction and eventually we come to a halt on the paved shoulder. Mom rests her head on the steering wheel, sobbing. "I wish I could have died. We should all be dead." Annette is still trying to soothe her. "It's okay Mom, we're okay." Mom backhands her in the face, furious. "You don't know anything. Shut up!"

Mom catches her breath, gets out of the car to check for visible damage. There is none. After a few moments outside, she gets back into the driver's seat and carries on, getting us back home. We are all silent. I don't take a full breath during the rest of that drive. My nine-year-old brain is trying to make sense of what just happened. Mom wants to kill herself? She wants us to die too?

*   *   *

Somehow all this walking is blurring the line between past and present. It's hard for me to tell what's real in each moment. I'm stuck in memory as if I'm on the road with volatile parents. Will my travelling companions stay with me on this journey? Will I stay with them?

When did we start living at such an emotional distance from each other? I keep wondering how we arrived at this juncture. Is there a moment when I stopped trusting? How can that be, when we've been so close? We hold each other's secrets. One thing I know for certain is that we have many shared values. When we started having our family, we both agreed on how we wanted to respect our children, and made commitments to be the parents we wanted to be. We have made difficult decisions about money, worked hard to make sure our family had what was needed. We've had many a discussion about allocating our limited financial resources, and how best to divide up workloads. We've laughed and cried together, celebrated successes and grieved our losses. Why is it so hard for us to make contact now?

How did I get here?

While I walk, my mind ponders these questions, painful as that may be, much like I probe a sore tooth in my mouth with my tongue. Checking—does it still hurt? Yes it does. Leave it alone for a while. Check again. Yup. Still hurts.

I am more than ready to stop by the time we arrive in Atapuerca, only to find there is no room at the only *refugio* in the village. A group of newly arrived pilgrims is lounging outside the entrance, and one of them, Fredric from Germany, recognizes us from last night. "We just took the last beds. There's no more space here and this is the only place to stay in town."

Once we have firmly established that there is no space for us, I take off at a blistering space, fuelled by anger. Now it's my turn! I can't stop thinking very unkind thoughts about everything to do with this trail. I grumble to myself as I walk-run down the trail: *Spring is not the high season for travellers on the Camino. Already the supporting services can't keep up with the demand. What a bunch of bullshit!* And: *Nobody told us the Camino would be over-run by Germans. They are so fit and athletic and they get up early and then we have to keep walking longer because they've filled up the places to stay.*

I attribute the German pilgrims as being the most aggressive to get into *refugios*. Even when I know it's not true, I relish my sense of self-righteousness. I channel my anger into walking faster to the next destination, so I can get this whole day over with. I don't care how far back my walking companions are, but they are both keeping up to me. Russell comments, "I love this pace." I think to myself, *If only you knew what was behind this, you wouldn't love it so much.*

My strategy works. We arrive at Olmos de Atapuerca, a little off the main Camino trail, in less than one hour. Our day has turned into a twenty-six kilometre half-marathon. There are beds for us here and I am so very grateful. It's been a cold, windy, rainy day on the outside, and a day full of fire and rain for our threesome. Given the emotional content of my day, I am now feeling quite discouraged and tired, yet relieved to have the walking finally over.

My mood improves dramatically once my pack and boots are off and I've had my shower. Our *refugio* is small, adjacent to a bar, so the services are within easy range. We decide to use the washing machine to clean our walking clothes but, as we've experienced in other *refugios*, after we put our money in, nothing happens. Russell goes to the person at the bar who is in charge of the *refugio*.

> Russell: "The washing machine isn't working. We put our money in, but it didn't start."
>
> Barman: "I guess it's not working."
>
> Russell: "So is there anything you can do to fix it?"
>
> Barman: "No, it's not working."

Back to hand-washing my dirty clothes. We vow not to bother using the washing machines on the Camino from now on. It seems a Spanish plot to get pilgrims to spend money, a low-end version of slot machines. The house always wins.

CHAPTER 16

MAY 1, DAY 13
OLMOS DE ATAPUERCA TO BURGOS
(18 KM)

I wake up feeling surprisingly rejuvenated this morning, ready to begin another day with a clean slate, and clean (albeit somewhat damp) clothing. Fortunately my merino wool shirt dries quickly as I walk, and I can hang my extra pair of hiking socks on my pack to dry as long as the day is sunny. Today promises to have some sun, although the wind persists.

We leave the *refugio* in a companionable silence. Although our trio walks in close proximity to each other, long periods of time go by before any one of us speaks. Mornings are when I most appreciate our quiet connection. It's when I get lulled back into the hypnotic rhythm of walking.

I deliberately chose not to bring any form of electronic device for listening to music since I prefer to have an internal soundtrack accompanying my footsteps. Songs tend to appear unbidden in my brain, in response to what I'm seeing, feeling or the pace of my walking. Lately I've been surprised by how many songs from the sixties and seventies are showing up. Maybe the old songs are linked to the ways my body seems to be releasing memories of me and my mother as I was growing up.

The musical playlist of my teen years living at home is inextricably woven with "She's Leaving Home" by the

Beatles. As is typical, I only remember song fragments, outlining one morning, the morning the young daughter leaves home. Parents asking, "Why would she leave us so thoughtlessly" ... "we gave her everything money can buy." The daughter "stepping outside is free. She's leaving home, bye bye." I often felt that I was given a lot of things that money could buy, and yet I felt so alone and unhappy. I felt like I'd been born into the wrong family. As a young teen I wished the boys would find me attractive, thinking that was the way I would finally have freedom and a place where I belonged.

*   *   *

I am thirteen, asking my mom, "Am I pretty?" She does not respond, and I keep asking. I really want to know. Finally, exasperated, and without my knowing it, she goes into my bedroom with her white lipstick and writes in large letters on the full-length mirror "Marie is ugly," accentuated by a cartoon drawing of a face with tongue sticking out. I feel sick to my stomach, like I've been punched in the gut when I see that message. I wring the tears out of my pillow that night, silently sobbing into its soft foam. The next day, I come to breakfast and act as if nothing unusual has happened. I ask Valentine what there is to bring for my school lunch today.

*   *   *

I can tell I'm in a melancholy mood when I hear song lyrics from "Eleanor Rigby" going around in my head. "All the lonely people, where do they all belong?" I asked myself that question as a teen, sharing a deep kinship with those who feel lonely. When I'm in a more rebellious frame of mind, early Bob Dylan tunes show up. I always loved the song, "Maggie's Farm." "I ain't gonna work on Maggie's Farm no more." What's he even doing on that farm? Those people are all treating him like shit! Like my family. Sing it Bob! "I ain't gonna work for Maggie's brother no more!"

On to Jimi Hendrix when I need something more raucous to keep me going. I hear guitar solos from "All Along the Watchtower" and "Purple Haze" running through my brain later in the day, when I've arrived at the trance state so reminiscent of my drug-altered experiences. One of the titles of a Jimi Hendrix album I owned is "Are You Experienced?" I would proudly pick up that album and each time answer the question with a yes. I am experienced. "Excuse me while I kiss the sky." I've been there. More than once.

And then a swift fast forward to the folk festival bands I have enjoyed over the past few years, remembering some of my favourite moments from day-time workshop stages at the Calgary Folk Festival. Another unforgettable live music mash-up from the Salmon Arm Roots and Blues Festival, where eleven musicians who had never played together before jammed for twenty-seven minutes. It was improvisation at its finest. Live music has magic and life and love. As one band I particularly enjoy has stated on stage, "Music can change the world."

Many hours go by when I am content with absorbing the sights and sounds around me. The external soundtrack of my pilgrimage has great richness and subtlety, like the sound of bells worn by domesticated animals in the fields next to the Camino route. I am alerted to the presence of pilgrims by what I hear. Many individuals use walking sticks, and those with metal tips make a sharp sound when they hit pavement or concrete—clack, clack, clack, clack, incessant and hard to ignore. Human sounds—pilgrim voices behind and approaching, volume increasing, beside us for brief greetings, then voices ahead and moving away, volume receding—the rhythm and cadence of different languages its own form of music. Workers in vineyards and fields sometimes call out to each other in the distance.

In the town squares we pass through there are often children playing soccer while parents look on, much laughter and excitement and conversation all taking place in the central gathering area. Occasionally there is a musician or two, either outside or in a bar. Church bells are also frequent audio companions. Every community larger than fifty people seems to have its own church, with a belfry and bells that ring before mass, at noon, and other times for no reason I can discern.

In some of the less developed areas, the path occasionally follows streams, so I feel lulled by the sound of water rushing over rocks, spilling over obstacles, on its way to join the sea. The stream sounds evoke a childhood memory.

*　　*　　*

In the springtime, Valentine takes us out of school to snare fish while they are spawning in the creeks. This is one of my favourite ways to spend time with Mom, along with any brothers and sisters willing to come. She wakes us up very early and we're piled into the car by 5:30. She packs copper snare wire, pliers, and a couple of hand-held fishnets, then we head out on the gravel back roads to a stream where Valentine has heard the fish are running. Often no one else is there yet, it's just us. I love the golden early morning light in the forest as we arrive, the sound of the rushing water, and the fresh green smell in the air, new sap from the trees rising with the warming of the air temperatures. All the winter snow has melted, and there is a new carpet of undergrowth, with some early blooming violets if I look carefully enough. Our first task is to spread out and scour the nearby forest to find a recently fallen tree branch big enough to handle the weight of a fish. A branch that's too old will snap easily and that's not good for our purposes.

Snaring is a simple way to catch fish when they're spawning, since they are heading upstream and often take time to rest in pools or close to the banks. With the loop of copper wire attached to the end of a branch, we sneak up behind resting fish and slip the loop of the snare over the tail and up to the middle of its body. Then with a quick lift and flip onto the bank, the fish is on shore, flopping away until I can remove the snare and toss the fish into the cooler half filled with ice that we have for storing our catch. When using the snare gets boring, I start wading in the creek along the edges of the bank, holding my hands steady in the water ahead of me. If I move slowly and carefully enough, I can bring my hands up alongside the gills of a fish without scaring it and use the gills to grab and toss it onto the shore. I'm proud of myself, that I'm able to catch so many fish this way. We haul out pickerel, perch and jackfish until we have enough. It doesn't take long.

What makes this time so special is that I know it's not legal for us to be catching fish in this way. I've heard Mom and Dad having arguments about her choice to keep going out to snare during spawning season, since Dad knows it will reflect badly on him if his wife gets caught breaking a law. But Valentine is defiant, and this is something she's been doing since she was a little girl. "No Fish and Game Officer is going to tell me what to do." And that's that. When Dad's away, Valentine likes to play and she takes me along as her partner in crime. I feel uneasy about what we're doing, but the sense of danger and adventure overrides any misgivings I might have.

When we get hungry or need a break, we can run to the cooler Mom has packed with sandwiches and fruit, or drink a cup of Red Rose tea from the thermos, the tea whitened with Carnation evaporated milk and sweetened with sugar in the same way that Valentine prepares her tea at home.

*   *   *

Valentine loved being outside, and she taught me to pay close attention to the natural world. I feel surprisingly connected to her as I walk here in Spain, like when I see familiar shapes of birds in flight and imagine Valentine's appreciation for creatures of this land. Like when I hear a sharp-pitched cry that alerts me to what I think is a raptor in the midst of scudding clouds blowing by. A soaring hawk or Spanish eagle? Memory and present-day merge into one.

On the road in front of me I spot a tiny, yellow-breasted bird. It flies up without making a sound. I hear the short "chips" of other birds in the forest underbrush, the new spring foliage rendering them invisible. Many creatures remain beautiful and un-named, as I slowly let go of my need to label. My day-to-day experience of spring continues to be a visual feast. A huge variety of spring flowers is emerging as we walk; we see the season unfolding each day. Some species are recognizable; I know when I am looking at an orchid, or a gentian, for example. Others are outrageous in their differences. All are breath-taking in their beauty. Light purple wildflowers adorn the roadside after we pass the village of Belorado. Numerous domesticated flowering shrubs liven up the exterior of the old stone buildings that we wander by. Wisteria blossoms with their large purple clusters hang across the building edges like a frame for the grey walls within. As we approach villages, often located on hillsides, deep purple irises, like sentinels, announce that civilization is nearby.

A highlight for this morning is walking on an alternate route, a cart track that takes us over a height of land before dropping down to rejoin the main Camino. For a time this morning it is just the three of us walking through a rocky hillside area, hearing only the occasional sound of a bell on a moving animal we do not see. The opportunity to be more isolated on this trip is a welcome one, and I keep laughing at myself as I discover how much I need to be solitary.

Silence and solitude have been surprisingly rare so far, not like the backpacking trails I am used to in North America. A many of our mountain treks we end up at campsites where the sight of five or six other tents seems like too many. One time our group of ten walked the Centennial Trail from Bedwell Lake on the east side of Vancouver Island over to Clayoquot Sound on the west side for a pick-up by water taxi. Our party was the only one travelling this rough route in early August. Our leader knew all the twists and turns of the very rough "troute"—a combination of trail and route—to get us to our final destination. We followed rocky creek beds, wandered through the old growth cedars, clambered over ridges and hillsides and old avalanche slopes. We hiked for six days without seeing another person until we got to our pick-up point at the ocean. The predominant sounds were wind in the trees, occasional bird songs, and water rushing over rocks.

When we rejoin the official pilgrim road it feels like a race. There are many more bodies and new faces on the trail, so my guess is that it's the long weekend crowd getting out and doing a section of the Camino. I don't like the frenzy of having to "get there" so we stop at a café in a small town along the way, ordering coffee and croissants as a second breakfast. This morning I am quite hungry so I'm happy for the extra fuel to walk into the city. We also buy two *bocadillos*, fresh buns with ham and cheese, along with apples for our lunch.

Approaching cities requires that we walk through industrial outskirts first, then suburbs and row housing, finally into the historic centre where the *refugios* are most often located. The routes into cities usually parallel busy highways, and traffic sounds are less meditative, often so loud they preclude thought and conversation. Our entrance into Burgos is no exception.

The closer we get to the city centre, the less intimate our journey feels. So far, as we walk the Camino, whenever we see people there is eye contact, a smile, a "*hola*" or a "*Buen Camino*" said in greeting as we pass each other. Now, the eye contact and greetings stop altogether. The fact that we are pilgrims who have walked into Burgos seems irrelevant to the lives of those we encounter.

The first hotel we try to check into is fully booked, since it is May 1, a Spanish holiday. We regroup by wandering over to one of the central squares in old downtown Burgos and pull out our lunch supplies. There is much to occupy us as we munch away on our sandwiches and fruit. May 1, we discover, is the European equivalent of Labour Day. There is a demonstration of some kind about labour in the plaza where we are sitting. I read something about Worker Solidarity. I see signs protesting child labour and the exploitation of children in the workplace. There is a No Nike poster as part of the display. Many people are milling about, although it's not quite a party atmosphere, rather more like strolling and promenading. We take in the sights and sounds happily taking the last bites of our apples.

We still need a place to stay so we check at the reception desk of a second hotel, which we are told is also full. However, this hotel owns a building directly across the street to handle overflow customers like us. It's more like a run-down apartment, but it's in the city centre where we want to be. We have our own bathroom, three beds, and a balcony. I move some furniture to one side to create more space for us and our gear. I consider putting the two single beds together to create a double bed for Rod and me. I'm starting to feel my desire for more physical contact with my husband, although I still hold back from initiating much. Cuddling at night would feel good, but bunk beds aren't great for two adult bodies. My body is getting more insistent about her need for physical touch, no matter what my mind might have to say. It's more internal push-pull, with my body saying "yes" to sensual contact and my mind holding on to resentment and grudges.

Sharing a room with Russell certainly puts the brakes on my desire, but that doesn't stop me from thinking about possibilities, and remembering times from early on. I couldn't keep my hands off Rod, and it seemed the same for him. Neither of us wanted to get out of bed in the morning to get ready for work, because more appealing options awaited in the horizontal realm. I have loved the feel of skin-to-skin, the smell of this man I am married to, the warmth that emanates from his body. He knows how to bring me to that place of ecstasy, slowly building tension, easing off, building again.

Instead of taking a cold shower, I step out onto the balcony to check out the view. It's too uncomfortable to spend much more than a few minutes out there, but my internal heat cools down to a manageable level.

I am grateful for the rest day we will be taking here, but already I have decided I don´t want to spend any extra time in other large population centres. Walking is where my heart is, not in the cities. I think we're all more comfortable on the road.

I'm anxious about buying our bus tickets, given the language limitations of the service industry people who don't speak much English, and ourselves, with our halting Spanish. I am counting on Rod to handle this transaction. *Buen Suerte* to him!

CHAPTER 17

MAY 2, DAY 14
BURGOS
(0 KM)
REST AND REFLECTION

A rest day! I wake early in order to take time for journal writing, a rare morning luxury on this walk. As I record my thoughts and feelings with pen to paper, I feel a sense of freedom and ease with words. How affirming, since I've been finding that the more time I spend on the trail, the longer it takes for me to come up with spoken words to express what's inside of me. That's in English! Then there's the fun of looking for equivalent words in Spanish, if I'm trying to speak with a local person. Sometimes I have no words in either language so I resort to gestures and pointing when all else fails. I occasionally observe some listeners rolling their eyes and shrugging shoulders as I do my best to make myself understood. At times, the eye rolling is mine, when I'm frustrated with my limitations. I'm not always aware of my body language and Rod is quick to point that out to me.

Rod: "Wow, did you ever treat that woman badly."

Me: "What?"

Rod: "Oh, come on, the way you were so dismissive, eyes rolling and walking away like that."

Me: "I didn't even know that's what I was doing."
His feedback shakes me up.

I can't help but wonder what gets in the way of expressing myself in another language. I can construct whole conversations in Spanish in my mind as I walk—it's one of the ways I occupy myself on the trail—but when it comes to opening my mouth to say something, it's like my throat seizes up and nothing comes out. I get angry at myself and I feel frustrated, and yet I haven't been able to push past that fear of making a mistake. I notice that even when I try to rehearse what I want to say, my brain kicks into overdrive, and I can't keep up with the flood of thoughts. It's easier not to say anything and yet this self-imposed silence is lonely. I miss female companionship and shared understanding, the unspoken resonance I have with Emma and my closest women friends.

Beyond my reluctance to say anything because I don't want to look or sound foolish it seems there is a bigger process going on. I'm spending so much time in silence as I walk, letting my mind roam around in non-linear space, trying to trap those impressions with words seems almost impossible. It's like trying to capture a flock of sparrows hopping about on the ground, chasing after the flitting bodies while they easily take flight and escape. Sometimes I am choosing to stay silent because what I have to say would be unkind, mean, or unpleasant. If it was just Rod and I travelling on our own, I might have unleashed unkind words earlier, but with Russell here, this isn't the time or place to let those feelings out. What purpose would it serve?

In my silence I'm practising focusing on what I love about where I am, rather than ruminating about all the things that are frustrating or that don't feel good. I'm pleasantly surprised that I can occupy my mind by concentrating on my surroundings, rather than continuously noticing the pain in my feet. I'm intrigued by how much this shift in focus is helping me to enjoy each day more. Maybe this is the pathway to making some of those changes I long for. Finally, when I've finished my writing time, we head out the door for big city adventures. Our pension is located near a number of sites that we want to visit, all within easy walking distance. Rod has a great suggestion, one I hadn't even considered. "Let's go to the farmer's market. It's just a few blocks away from where we're staying. I looked it up online yesterday and it should be a good one to check out." So off we go. We spend a couple of hours at the market, sampling vendor wares, allowing ourselves time to examine each display. In the midst of the novelty and abundance, my concerns about food are non-existent. I had no idea that so many types of cheeses are produced here in Spain—sheep, goat, cow, combinations of all three. We see meat prepared in a variety of states, large sides of beef and pork hanging from hooks, display cases with ground meat and cubes of lamb, beef, pork, and goat. Whole chickens, chicken parts, and innards. Sausages, spicy salamis, and chorizos. There is so much to choose from. After many samples we finally purchase an aged hard cheese made from sheep's milk that will carry well in our packs for tomorrow. For today's lunch we choose a softer goat cheese. To round out our meals, we find some hearty whole wheat bread, and pick up some spicy dry sausage, the kind that will last for a few days without refrigeration.

At the fruit section, the variety on display invites me to touch. But I quickly discover touching is not allowed. The one time I try to pick up an apple, the vendor scolds me, and points to the sign—*No Tocar Las Frutas*—No Touching The Fruit. Instead, when I ask for an apple, the vendor takes her time, lovingly it seems, to choose what she thinks is the best one for me.

I briefly remember those apple cores I forced myself to eat just a few years ago, wishing my pain would come to a swift end. Now, here in this farmer's market in Spain, I am amazed at the joy I feel as I wait to hold the ruby red piece of fruit in my hand.

The action of buying fruit becomes a personal, intimate exchange. After that first scolding, I manage to hold my hands away from any other tempting offerings. We add more oranges and apples to the weight of our packs, all carefully selected by whoever is in charge of the display.

Breakfasts are often served at each *refugio*. However, some places only offer basic hard bread and jam. On a good day there might be some yogurt, and on a great day, some diced-up fruit. We stop frequently at *cafés* in the late morning for baked goods or Spanish tortilla— which is like a potato and egg omelet—to supplement the breakfasts provided for pilgrims. Here in the Burgos market, I am looking for breakfast foods to augment the usual pilgrim offerings. I find a jar of sesame butter, or tahini, which is most often used to prepare spreads like hummus, with a chick-pea base. I plan to use the tahini as a spread on my morning toast or dry crusty bread. We also find a small bag of granola and some plain yogurt. Familiar foods are comforting reminders of home.

Buying what we want for breakfasts and lunches gives me a small sense of control over what I consume, since my anxiety about food and the amounts I eat never quiets down completely. Even on this trip, when I'm walking so much every day, I worry about gaining weight. Since we've started picking up baked treats from the bakeries and cafes along the way, I feel even more anxious. It's a double-edged sword. I love how we are indulging ourselves and relaxing into the rhythm of our walking. Then guilt kicks in about how I'm eating too much. I hear a constant nagging voice in my head.

More often than not, that voice sounds like my mother.

"You're too fat," I hear her say. "You're letting yourself go. Do you have any idea how many calories are in that croissant?"

It's as if I can't win.

I might very well be the one pilgrim who is heavier at the end of her walk than she was at the beginning. It doesn't help that I'm always judging myself by how I look when I see my reflection in a mirror or in the shop windows as I pass by. The judgment is inevitably harsh.

No matter what my weight is, I always think I'm too fat. That constant nagging voice in my head reminds me.

Look at that extra layer you're carrying.

You've got love handles.

You've let yourself go.

Valentine used to refer to herself as having a "pot belly," even when she was very thin. She was always concerned about her food intake, and she often would say things like, "I'm so fat," when she probably never weighed more than 110 pounds. My mother was 5'4". This is not fat!

* * *

I'm seven, looking at a black and white photograph of Valentine as a young woman, standing on the bridge over Kaufmann Creek. She's wearing a dark knee-length dress and a short coat with a fur collar. "Look at my stove pipe legs." I don't see them. Were they hiding under that dress? Would I get them one day? Should I be worried? Whenever Mom looked at that picture, that was the one thing she said. "Look at my stove pipe legs."

Was Mom looking at her body through a fun house mirror?

I'm thirteen. I'm self-conscious and embarrassed by my changing body. I'm not much interested in the latest trends in clothing, but Mom loves to read fashion magazines and keep up with the American celebrity culture. People magazines lie in a stack on the table beside our living room sofa. She longs to have a daughter that is as interested in the latest clothing trends as she is. I'd rather find blue jeans that fit, comfortable tops, and baggy sweaters to hide within. As Mom flips through the latest Vogue, she looks up at me and says, "It's too bad you're not tall and willowy like Twiggy." What can I say? My ever-sensitive mind is stunned into numbness. Her comment feels like a sharp slap to the side of my head.

*   *   *

Recalling adolescent Marie still living with Valentine, it's hard to look forward to eating my lunch. But as we take our food purchases and head over to a green space nearby, the sun is shining, and my mood shifts. We find an unoccupied bench to sit on. Outdoorsy Canadians that we are, we'd rather eat in the park than go inside a smoky café or bar for our mid-day meal. We get out pocket knives to slice the dry spicy salami and spread the goat cheese over rough slices of bread, happily chewing away at our farmer's market bounty. Crunchy carrots add texture to the feast. Fresh apples from the scolding vendor round out our simple meal. I'll save the dark chocolate I bought for our afternoon snack. Right now I've left my food worries behind. I'm in a small version of heaven: a full stomach, sandals on my feet, and more time left for exploring this historic city.

We amble along in search of more modern city attractions. Russell managed to find comic book stores in Logrono, and Burgos doesn't disappoint. He seems mesmerized by the shelves of books and graphic novelists he knows aren't available in Canada. I keep learning more about Russell as he shares this passion with me. Rod hangs out on the periphery of the store. I think he's waiting for our shopping lust to calm down so we can go visit the historic sites on our list—the Burgos Cathedral and the old castle. That will please his archaeologist heart, I'm sure.

I'm surprised by my desire to look at clothing and

fashion. I can't stop staring at shoes and boots the women
are wearing. Fancy boots are standard every-day wear. I
have seen more styles of footwear than I ever could have
imagined. My dormant love of shoes has been reignited
as I walk around these streets. Perhaps there is a shopping
spree in my future, once I'm finished carrying everything
on my back. Barcelona, here I come!

Wandering the narrow cobblestone streets toward
the Cathedral, we begin to hear the strains of music and
the swelling noise of cheering. Drawn in by the sound of
celebration, we round a corner and find ourselves caught
up in the swirl of a festival. Every day is a festival somewhere
in this country. Twirling female dancers arrayed in colourful
skirts of scarlet etched with black, white tunics in sharp
contrast to the brilliant reds. The men wear black pants with
white shirts, green sashes draped over their shoulders.
The dancers move in an exuberant pattern, the pace set
by a group of musicians possibly revved up by caffeine.
Arms raised, the swirling dancers gracefully move in
and out of the centre of their circle, the appreciative
crowd clapping and roaring approval. The old buildings
lining the street are as colourful as the dancers, dark red
facades adjacent to walls of golden yellow and deep
orange. The colours of Spain. We join in the laughing,
cheering, clapping crowd, smiling broadly at each other
and the faces around us.

Gradually the entire procession moves on up the
street, as we make our way to the Burgos Cathedral, in the
middle of the city. Building of this church began in the
13th century, with several additions creating tall narrow
spires, monumental arches, and large doorways. In 1984,
the cathedral was designated a UNESCO World Heritage
site. At the time of our visit, a major restoration of the
exterior is underway, but the scaffolding and nets don't
diminish the majesty of this structure. It's hard to take it
all in, and our cameras are not capable of photographing
the entire edifice. I buy postcards instead, once we enter

the building. In order to get inside, we have to make our way around the shabbily dressed beggar woman who sits on the concrete, scarf-covered head bowed so her face is not visible, hands outstretched for whatever money visitors might spare. The sight of a beggar at a church entrance has become familiar. And I'm uncertain about how to respond to those outstretched hands. One part of me knows that it's best to donate to an organization that serves the homeless and the poor. The other feels completely heartless as I walk by the ragged clothes and bowed head. What is the role of giving and generosity here? As a pilgrim, should I be more generous? I have no easy answers.

We stamp our own *Credencial* at the entry to the Cathedral, and follow the self-guided instructions that appear in many languages, English included.

From there it's a short meander to the ruins of the Burgos Castle. It's located on the highest point of land in the city. This historic site has an interesting story dating back to around 800 AD. Napoleon occupied the castle during his campaign, and when he lost the battle of Waterloo he blew up the building. Talk about a poor sport! Russell has a friend who likes to blow things up, and I now imagine Napoleon as a smaller-framed version of Russell's friend. We laugh together as I share this image with Rod and Russell.

After our time roaming the city, I speak up. "I've been thinking. Let's not spend any extra time in León. We can get to Ponferrada in one day, without having to stop over. That will give us more time on the trail." Russell's eyes light up. "I'd rather be walking than be a tourist in a city." Rod adds, "It's less expensive on the trail. I'm happy to skip León." I'm surprised and relieved that I don't have to go through the slice and dice routine. The next thing I know, Russell asks for our guidebook. I hand it over to him, and he scans the description of León. "We'll miss some famous landmarks, but so what."

Rod agrees. "This is a good choice."

I'm so relieved. The way I feel right now, I don't need to see more monuments, churches, castles, or other historic buildings. This journey is about the walking, the exchanges with people along the way, noticing the details in the landscape around me, and careful observation of my internal reality. I let the men know, "Quite honestly, I'm not waiting with anticipation to see the next shrine or worship at the next altar."

Far from it.

CHAPTER 18

MAY 3, DAY 15
BURGOS TO LEÓN
*
LEÓN TO PONFERRADA
(241 KM)

Plan for the day: Early rise. Walk to bus station. Buy tickets for the 6:35 a.m. bus from Burgos to León. Two-hour stopover in León. Eat breakfast. Bus to Ponferrada.

We easily find the bus station, given that we wandered into that area of the city yesterday. I let Rod handle the purchase of bus tickets, feeling a bit guilty that I don't step up to speak Spanish more often. I appreciate that Rod is so capable with speaking another language. It seems like he's more outgoing now that we're traveling, more willing to engage in conversations with Spanish and French speakers whenever he has the chance. At home he can be quite reclusive. It's as if we've done a role reversal. At home I'm more likely to be the one who is social and talks a lot. Here? I tend to hide behind Rod's willingness to communicate.

So here I am, sitting in the lap of luxury on the ALSA bus line, our carrier for the day. The seats are comfortable, widely spaced, the seat backs can be adjusted for a comfortable sleeping position. There's a bathroom which I will probably need before we get to León. As we zoom along the highway, I reflect on how different this is from the Greyhound bus rides I've had in Western Canada, some of which had faint smells of vomit in the back rows. Male passengers sometimes tried to pick me up on the long-distance rides, especially the overnights, like the Calgary to Vancouver run. My willingness to talk was interpreted as interest in something more, and there were times I received unwelcome physical advances. One man even said to me in very angry tones, "You're a fraud" as if he deserved to fondle me because we'd had a conversation. "Get a grip buddy. Not in this lifetime!" I did not let myself fall asleep that night even though I sat as close to the driver as possible.

Most of the people around me are snoring. It's like being in a portable *refugio*. There are some sections along the highway that look as barren as southern Alberta with coulees and some green grasses, shrubbery, rocky outcrops and piles of stones. Then the buildings in the small villages jar me back into the awareness that I am in Spain, not Alberta. Such an ordinary thing, to be riding a bus. But not so ordinary in Spain.

In León we have a two hour layover before our connection leaves for Ponferrada. It's a good time to have our breakfast. As we're eating, I look up and see a woman with a Canadian Company of Pilgrims crest sewn on her backpack. I don't hesitate to make contact. I go up to her and ask, "Are you from Canada?" Her face lights up. "Yes," she responds, and the conversation continues from there. She and her husband join us for the rest of our break. "We're from Deline in the Northwest Territories. It's on Great Bear Lake, north of Yellowknife," he tells us. "I'm originally from England," she says. "I was posted as a nurse there and I've never left." He was born and raised in the area, a Dene man who has often been interviewed for Traditional Land Use studies. I have worked with Dene people in northern Alberta, south of the Northwest Territories. I have probably interviewed relatives of this man. The conversation flows easily and two hours pass quickly. As I board the bus once again, I wonder, "What were the odds that I would meet a Dene man at a bus station in Spain?"

From León, we are whisked by bus through time and space, bypassing the Meseta. Everything I've heard and read about this section, which we are speeding through on wheels, not feet, suggests that it is a challenging landscape that offers little relief from the elements. When I gaze out the window I can see hikers with their packs at points where the trail parallels the road we're on. I've heard that the roads were built to deliberately follow the Camino route. This obviously wasn't a choice made by pilgrims. It doesn't create the greatest experience for a walker to have vehicles of all sorts rushing by. And now I'm on one of those motorized beasts.

When we arrive in Ponferrada, we have to walk from the bus station to the *refugio*. It turns out our home for the night is a little harder to find than we expected, since we are not on a Camino route with the scallop shell markers. We ask for directions at a newsagent kiosk, and a fight almost breaks out as the local patrons compete to give us information.

Most of this exchange takes place in Spanish, with Rod doing his best to ask questions and understand the answers. Russell and I are carefully observing, trying to pick up what we can from the scene in front of us.

> Rod asking the man in the kiosk: "Do you know how to get to the pilgrim *refugio* from here?" (He gets out a guidebook and points to the description of where we want to go.)

> Man not looking too confident: "I think it's that way." (He points in a direction.)

> Woman standing beside us: "No, that's not where it is. You have to go this way." (She points in a different direction.)

Second man in the crowd, in a loud voice: "You don't know what you're talking about! It's over there!" (He points in yet a different direction.)

Suddenly everyone has an opinion, and a large, vocal group coalesces around the kiosk, everyone talking at once, gesturing, pointing at us, then away to some part of the city. We watch, bewildered, not sure what is being said and hoping for the best. I wonder if they'd notice if we just slipped away. However, before that can happen, one man is designated as the envoy for the group. He comes over and gives us a few directions we can follow, at least until we need to ask someone else. We depart, still not sure if we're headed toward the *refugio*, but we have to put our trust somewhere.

After more than one hour of walking, we finally see the Camino scallop shell markers which lead us to our pilgrim home for the night. This *refugio* has rooms that accommodate up to six people—three sets of bunk beds—in a fairly new building, a well-landscaped inner courtyard, and inviting sunshine. However, even with a warm welcome from the *hospitaleros*, I feel out of synch. I haven't walked the Meseta, so I do not have that pilgrim experience to share. I feel uprooted, transplanted. It is hard for me to find a compatible energetic fit with those around me particularly since we have left behind the familiar people that we've been meeting off and on throughout the early stages. Newly formed bonds with fellow travellers have been severed. There are no welcoming smiles here, and my time on the trail has already moved me to an inward focus. I don't have much energy for making new connections. My sense of companionship with other pilgrims has vanished. The natural rhythm of my journey has been interrupted in every way.

My sense of who I am on this journey is shaken

again. I know taking the bus has was the right decision from every practical viewpoint. But to be honest, I feel somewhat ashamed that I haven't walked the whole distance to get to Ponferrada. On some level, I'm expecting that I'm going to be called out as a fraud. Yet once I arrive, I'm allowed into the *refugio*. I'm not excluded from sharing bunk bed dormitory rooms with other pilgrims, no matter how I got here. Our decision to use buses to get from Burgos to Ponferrada has forced me to realize that—even though I never imagined this would happen—I have developed some ideas about "Marie as pilgrim." Without my conscious awareness, a gradual transition has been happening. Along with my many sense impressions and silent musings along the trail are thoughts about how I am travelling, and what constitutes a "proper pilgrim." I'm intrigued by how I am so prone to judge and rank things like people's behaviour, choices, and lifestyle. Here on the Camino, it shows up in terms of how I judge people who are choosing to take taxis to their next stop, rather than walk the whole way. I look down on those who send their packs or luggage on to the next *refugio*, so they are able to walk with light day packs. It's how I think less of the people who are choosing to stay in hotels every night. And it's how I judge pilgrims who are eating at high-end restaurants, choosing the best food and wine every night, when as a proper pilgrim, I believe that the only supper meal option for me to choose is the *Menu del Dia*.

Once we have registered, gotten our *Credencials* stamped, and settled into our assigned room, we head out the door. Our plan is to explore around the *Castillo de los Templarios* built in the 13th century. Our guidebook describes the Castle of the Templars as "a grand, triple-ramparted, fairy-tale castle." It was originally constructed to protect pilgrims from bandits. Our hopes for roaming around inside the castle are quickly dashed as we encounter large locked doors at the entrance-way. The adjoining

Basilica is also closed to visitors on Sunday afternoons. Apparently the Spanish have a different schedule for operating historic sites than we do in Canada, since weekends are usually peak times for visitors. The well-worn path around the castle walls suggests we're not the first people to have been turned away by the locked doors. We entertain ourselves by wandering around the perimeter of the castle walls and speculate about what we are finding.

> Rod: "Look at those turrets! They remind me of chess pieces – the rook."

> Marie: "That's funny, because I was thinking it looks like the castle at the beginning of the Wonderful World of Disney television show I used to watch as a kid. Keep your eyes peeled for fairies and rainbows overhead."

> Russell: "It seems like there should be a dragon inside. Or maybe a princess in one of the towers, waiting to be rescued."

> Chorus: "Rapunzel, Rapunzel, let down your hair."

> Me: "Russell, maybe you should go up in the tower and let down your long hair. We could turn the story around, and you could be the young man who is rescued by a strong woman."

As I assess the stone construction of the gigantic walls Rod guesses, "These walls must be at least four storeys high." It is magnificent, even if we don't have a chance to explore inside the walls. It takes us almost two hours to navigate the exterior, and when we're done, we're starting to feel hungry. We have learned not to ignore those hunger pangs so we switch our focus to finding a restaurant. As we saunter along the old cobblestone streets, we can tell when we are approaching a restaurant by the menu posted on the wall beside the entrance. One particularly amusing menu grabs our attention. It's written in Spanish, with the English translation underneath.

Rod: "Hey, check out this *Primero*. The first course is called *Caldo Bierciano*. And the English translation is Typical broth of the Bierzo. That's really helpful."

Me: "I'm more interested in the *Revuelto de Verduras*. Well, actually, I'm more interested in the English version: In a mess of vegetables. Doesn't that sound appetizing?"

Russell: "Well, if I'm going to order from here, I'd like to know what *Dorado a la Plancha* is. All it says for the translation is Gold to the Plate. What the heck is that?"

Rod: "I think we should keep looking. This restaurant looks a bit pricey at 15 euros for the *Menu del Dia*."

Me: "And the translations seem sketchy. Makes me wonder about the quality of the food."

Russell: "I'm easy. Whatever you think is fine with me."

Fortunately no one in our trio is ravenous at this point, otherwise the conversation might have gone a little less amicably. We amble up and down a few more streets, looking into gift shops and clothing stores until we end up sitting at an outside café, ordering yet another version of *Menu del Dia*. As our server arrives, he plunks down a bottle of local white wine onto the table. Then we order from the limited options. The *Primero* gives us the choice of either a soup or salad. As usual, the soup is bean and kale-based. The salad offerings are either pasta or potato. I have learned that these will probably arrive with plenty of mayonnaise. The *Segundo* is meat or fish with an accompaniment of French fries—with mayonnaise. By now I anticipate that when I order fish, it's likely to be oily and salty.

Such offerings along the pilgrim route have probably evolved to serve the needs of the large numbers of walkers, and the quality varies from place to place. Food options are a reflection of what is commonly available to local people in northern Spain, and it is nothing fancy. Learning to read a Spanish menu has me on a constant learning curve; sometimes I order, thinking a particular item will be arriving, only to find that in fact, it is another version of oily, salty fish. Or a mayonnaise-covered item.

The final course is *Postre*. Dessert, once again, is either flan or fresh fruit, along with coffee. The first time Russell ordered fruit for dessert, a single unpeeled orange was delivered in a bowl. The three of us burst out laughing, and I had to get out my camera. There are few, if any, embellishments on the *Menu del Dia*.

No matter what the options, I always choose the menu of the day, since it is the least expensive. It also reduces the need to make decisions. It's not all bad. I especially love the litre of wine that is automatically placed on the table as the server comes to take our order. Tonight when the wine arrives, another memory shows up, one that I wish would have stayed trapped in my cell membranes.

* * *

After the yelling between Mike and Valentine stops, Dad downs a 26-ounce bottle of Crown Royal whiskey, slams the empty bottle on a counter edge in the laundry room, smashing that corner of the counter. The bottle remains intact, even as it falls to the floor. Dad passes out on our dining room floor shortly afterwards. My younger brother and I hear him fall and emerge from where we've been secretly watching to help him out. We have never seen anyone passed out before, at least not in our home. Valentine is sitting in the La-Z-Boy chair, looking like a stone statue. We think Dad is dying, so we do our best to move him to his bedroom. That is impossible, given that he weighs well over 250 pounds and we are only twelve and ten years old.

I'm frantic, "We need to call for help. Should we phone the police?"

Mom barks out a dismissive laugh and speaks in a very cold manner, "He's not sick or dying. He's drunk. Just leave him be."

We eventually cover Dad up with a blanket and slink off to our respective bedrooms.

I feel ashamed and scared at the same time. I've only seen drunken people passed out on our town's main street, outside the hotel bar. Will Dad end up like that? My mother seems truly heartless. My mind races in anxiety.

If she treats Dad that way, what about me? What about the rest of us?

Later on in the night, when I go out to check, my father is no longer on the floor. There is never any mention of Dad's drinking again. Nothing. Silence. I never talk about it with my brother either. That night vanishes, along with all the other hard-to-explain bizarre unspeakable events that happen in our house. The only evidence that remains is that broken corner of the counter top in the laundry room.

*   *   *

I'm a long way from that living room as I lean into the warmth of the sun still beaming down on us. It's a refreshing change from the cold, windy wet weather we have had for the past several days. I have come to value the time that we spend sharing our supper meal, enjoying the wine-fuelled conversations that fill the gaps as we finish eating the first course and contentedly await delivery of the second to our table.

Me: "I still can't get over the fact that we met a Dene man in León, in the bus station. Plus he's been interviewed for Traditional Land Use studies. That seems like a one in a million chance."

Rod: "Yeah, that's pretty wild. I'm just happy I asked for the right bus tickets, and we ended up where we wanted to go."

Me: "I am so grateful that you are able to handle those transactions. I admire how you just step up and start talking. Especially when you often hold back when we're at home."

Rod: "I know. I like speaking in Spanish. It's part of the adventure."

Russell: "I'm glad that both of you know enough Spanish to get around, and I don't have to try and say much. It would be nice to have some other people my age to talk to, though."

Me: "You know, one option for you is to walk faster, and go at your own pace. Then you would be more likely to meet up with others and start up some friendships. We could arrange a meeting point where we all join up again. You don't have to stick with your parents."

Russell: "Actually that's not very appealing. I have a hard enough time talking to people in English, at home, let alone here on the trail. I'm going to stick with you guys."

Me: "It would have made a big difference to have Emma come along. Then the two of you could have gone off and had some of your own adventures."

Russell: "I'm not sure how adventurous either of us would be here. Neither of us is very outgoing. But I do miss spending time with her. She's easy to talk to, and we could at least create new board games or fantasy novel ideas while we walk."

And then our conversation rambles off into the territory of what we have experienced today, punctuated by silent periods of staring off into the distance.

Our slow, easy interaction throughout the meal is unlike our Canadian way of getting through supper as soon as possible, the meal almost an inconvenient interruption in the flow of our busy lives. At home my time is tightly scheduled and I'm often on the move; my meals are more like pit stops throughout my day, before I go on to the next activity. Meals are seldom events in and of themselves. In Spain, however, the pace is very different and we don't have anywhere to go after our meal other than back to our dormitory for the night, sharing space with a room full of other people.

As I stare off into the distance, I reflect on my role as a parent. I love that Russell and Emma like to spend time with each other. I know so many families where brothers and sisters keep their distance. My siblings and I still tend to avoid each other. Our times of getting together feel more like obligation rather than something I look forward to. I continue to be amazed that our son chose to walk with us, his parents, for this length of time. And for the most part, we are getting along. In fact, his presence is helping me to find a place of peace inside myself. Russell has been affirming what I see, supporting me when I'm feeling outweighed by Rod's opinions.

And at the same time, he is a supportive presence for Rod. How did I manage to raise such a son? After all that time and effort I put into learning how to be a respectful parent, this is the best that I could ask for. In fact, this relationship with my son is more than I ever could have imagined when I first held him in my arms.

When it is time to return to our *refugio*, I am in a peaceful, contented state of mind. Ponferrada is adjacent to a mountain range, and where we are staying is close to the outskirts of the city. Our views from here are stunning, snow-capped mountains reminding me of the Canadian Rockies I know so well.

My falling asleep thoughts are imagining Rod's body beside me, cuddling, leading to hands on bare skin, comfort growing to passionate heat, contentment building to excitement. Oh what our bodies could do if we were in a private room, in Ponferrada, in Spain.

CHAPTER 19

MAY 4, DAY 16
PONFERRADA TO
VILLAFRANCA DEL BIERZO
(25 KM)

We resume walking along a gravel track, away from the main highway, alternating between poplar-evergreen forests and vineyards on mountain hillsides. We are now in the highlands of El Bierzo, province of Léon. Apparently we have also crossed into white wine country, so we will have the opportunity to try out new varieties at dinner.

Last night in Ponferrada, the two people sleeping in the top bunks of our room were restless and left the room several times. It made for a poor night of sleep and I am weary today. Digestion problems abound for Russell; he is making frequent stops. Rod seems to be unaffected so he walks quite far ahead of us. He remembers to turn around occasionally, making sure we are still in sight.

Even though I'm tired and moving at a slow pace, I am grateful that Rod is walking ahead of me today. We were sticking closely together in Burgos and on the bus ride, to the point that I found Rod's commentary on our physical surroundings quite an interruption to the dreamy flow of my thoughts.

"Look at that billboard. It's for Nike."

"Barcelona, 600 km."

He loves reading signs aloud. I'm not sure when this started, maybe when the kids were small. Our son is now twenty years old. I want to shout, "WE CAN READ!" I recall the May 1 event in Burgos. There were many signs and Rod took the time to read each of them aloud in the language they were written in—some English, some Spanish. There was one that was all statistics—maybe it was about the numbers of labourers in Spain, in Burgos, in the province, breaking it out into males, females, apparently assigning numbers to categories of adults. Rod patiently and persistently read aloud to the end of the poster or billboard. I found something else to occupy my mind while he finished. I intended to check in with Russell about this—does he notice it too? Maybe he enjoys the read-aloud time.

I don't want to hear a running commentary of facts and history of our surroundings. This is not the realm I'm interested in these days. I'm so ready at times to vent my frustration, especially when I long to speak of my emotional experiences here on the trail. Early on in our relationship, Rod was able to listen to me at length as I shared strong feelings. At the same time I was fascinated by his encyclopedic knowledge. *Does Rod want to walk away from conversations about emotions as much as I do when I hear lists of facts?* Maybe this difference between us is as much about the way men and women in our culture are socialized. I keep longing for a female-to-female quality of conversation with my husband. It's not fair to him, or to me. I can't help but wonder, *How long has this been the quality of my relationship?*

I don't often hear the words "Thank you," even when I make arrangements, or problem-solve a difficult tangle. Instead I am asked about a detail I know nothing about, and our conversations end with me saying, "I don't know. If you want to know that, I guess you better ask." Sometimes I retort with unkind words, my voice sharp and critical. I wonder how the accumulation of my harsh responses may have trained Rod to be cautious about showing tenderness or kindness toward me.

It might be time to find some middle ground between absolute silence and impatient reaction.

I am seeing other quirky traits about my partner of twenty-five plus years. How he seems to be afraid to enter a building with a closed door. "That *mercado* won't be open," he'll say to us. Without testing whether that's true, he prepares to move on. I need to check it out for myself.

"Hey, we can get our lunch supplies here," I call over my shoulder as I enter the store. I've never before noticed his reluctance to try opening a closed door.

Probably the most difficult communication challenge I have with Rod is being pushed to rationalize and defend every statement I make. I think Rod plays the devil's advocate as a way to find things to say. He seems to enjoy pointing out the exceptions to statements I make. Maybe it's part of his academic training. But I'm not a student sitting in his classroom. I'm his wife, trying to share something from my heart, in my own clumsy way. It can be something as simple as, "I'm grateful for the cafés we stop at along the Camino. I enjoy the bold, rich taste of the dark roast coffee."

Rod inevitably replies with something like, "Well there was one place we stopped at where the coffee wasn't very good, maybe in Pamplona. They over-charged us too. I think they're ripping off the pilgrims."

Me: "Are there any places you think have served good coffee?"

Rod: "Well, most of them have been pretty good. I just didn't like that one in Logrono."

What I am really trying to say is how much I'm enjoying the way we are pacing out our days with coffee stops. When I hear about the exception, I hear Rod suggesting there is something wrong with my observation. The other type of response I get often involves an explanation.

Me: "There's a surprising number of pilgrims from Asia on this route. I never expected to see people from South Korea or Japan on the Camino."

Rod: "Well it makes perfect sense to me, because (insert lecture here)."

This shuts me down. Why can't he just say, "I've been noticing that too. How do you think all these people have heard about the Camino?" And then I could reply with whatever thoughts I have on the matter. That would be a conversation, not a lecture. I'm longing for emotional attunement, but what I get is a head-centred comment.

Yes, there are times I am feeling frustration toward my partner. And there are other times I am full of appreciation for everything he brings to our travel together. Russell is attuned to both Rod and me. He easily communicates with the two of us, speaking and listening in ways that honour our individual styles. How does he do that? I have much to learn from my adult son.

Birdsong finally draws my attention to my surroundings. All day long I hear birds singing and calling to each other. The many warblers I observe, likely different species, flit about in shades of yellow. Storks guard their large messy nests high in towers and church spires. They are obviously tending eggs or chicks. I'm surprised to see storks also feeding in the fields.

There are so many more people on the trail now, some of them with packs so tiny I wonder why they bother to carry anything. I feel totally jealous as I haul my 50-litre pack around. And yet, should the weather turn foul, which it is known to do here, I want to have all the proper gear. So I carry everything, and take more time getting places.

Our home tonight is another comfortable *albergue* with a room for just the three of us. Hopefully this will allow us to have a better night´s sleep. I catch myself getting excited as I anticipate sleeping in a room with no snoring. My excitement is short-lived. Rod snores loudly. My tactic is to fall asleep before he does, reading aloud from Billy Collins as my final act before shutting down for the night.

"To a Stranger Born in a Distant Country Hundreds of Years from Now."

CHAPTER 20

MAY 5, DAY 17
VILLAFRANCA DEL BIERZO TO
VEGA DE VALCARCE
(16 KM)
(YIN AND YANG OF THE CAMINO)

After breakfast this morning in the *refugio*, it doesn't take long for us to leave behind the scattered houses of Villafranca del Bierzo, quickly arriving at the intersection between the (less strenuous, safer) Low Route and the (more challenging) High Route. Given the good weather and our love of hiking in the Canadian mountain high country, our decision is made quickly. It's the High Route for us. The elevation gain starts almost immediately as the High Route traverses upward away from the old Camino trail, which parallels the highway. The day is clear and sunny, the track takes us into beautiful montane country with new wildflower species and vegetation. Just like there is a *Menu del Dia*, it seems there are *Flores del Dia*. Today I walk alongside an entire hillside covered with purple lavender, huge masses similar to what I have seen around our homes in Courtenay. I also spy yellow and white gorse and purple heather, along with other white and yellow flowers that are so numerous I stop trying to identify them. This glorious riot of colour fills me with joy. As a special bonus we have fewer pilgrims to share the trail with and great views into the surrounding valleys once we climb high enough. This is the "Yin," or *fantastico* part of the day.

On this second day out from Ponferrada, I have re-entered a trance state, a between-the-worlds place where I walk as one with the flowers, the smells, the blue sky, and everything else I observe around me.

It's a space where words show up in my brain more slowly, one at a time, not like the rapid strings of thought I'm used to when I'm at home. In my trance-like state I feel more of my mother's emotional history. Maybe it started before her, with her ancestors. From what I've been able to piece together, I suspect my mother felt a lot of disappointment, betrayal, and rage in her relationship with Mike. I witnessed many of their fights, heard the accusations thrown back and forth in loud and angry voices, felt myself scurry to whatever nearby hiding place I could find since there was no safety in those yelling voices, getting louder and ever more threatening, each one aggressively trying to win, out-posturing the other. Like the time Dad comes home after travelling for several weeks.

*   *   *

While Dad's been away, Mom and our grandfather, Cé, have been running the movie theatre owned by our family. Every Sunday after the weekly ritual of attending Catholic mass, my family gathers around our big kitchen table and we count the money from ticket and concession sales. Each denomination of currency is stored in a small white popcorn bag. The green one dollar bills are separated from the orangey-brown two dollar bills—this was before the one- and two-dollar coins were minted in Canada—blue fives and purple tens each in their own bags. Twenties get added to any fifties that might be in the weekly take. It's not a very sophisticated system, but it works well enough. Dad has only been home for a day before he checks in with Valentine.

Dad: "Where's the money from the theatre? I need to bring all that cash to the bank."

Mom: "There hasn't been enough money lately. I'm not telling you where I've got everything stored."

Dad: "You have to give it to me, that's from the business!"

Mom: "No I don't. I work hard to keep that theatre going while you're off gallivanting around. I owe you nothing!"

Their voices rise, neither one backing down. My younger brother and I are lurking on the edges of this drama, not sure how this is going to play out.

Valentine declares, "I'll burn that money before I hand it over to you!"

There's a sound of quick footsteps and rushing around in the house, then the back door slams as Mom heads to the edge of our yard where the burning barrel sits. Mom and Dad are past the point of talking or even yelling. I peek out the back window, watching what's happening with our parents. I secretly hope I can retrieve whatever riches I can from the barrel once this fight is over. It seems too dangerous, so I don't watch for long. Last thing I want is to get caught watching a big fight like this one.

When I do a thorough check of the backyard later, including looking through the contents of the burning barrel, there is no evidence of any dollar bills, of any denomination.

What was that all about? I wonder.

The Mike and Val relationship dynamic is strongly influenced by the ways that Mike, the sole son, has been raised in his Italian family as "the king." Others exist to serve him, his wife included. She is not treated as an equal, even though Valentine is a very smart, sensitive woman. There are few thank yous for all that Valentine does to support her husband and children. Mike, as de facto monarch, is often disrespectful towards Valentine, and buying lavish gifts for her does not erase the day-to-day build-up of hurt and disappointment.

Mike takes on work that requires longer periods of time away from home, and Mom is left alone to care for their large family. She does her best to keep up the pretense that he is being faithful to her. I'm probably thirteen years old when Mom starts wearing a blonde wig. She's always been a brunette. When her hair started to go grey she began using Clairol hair colour to keep the grey away. So what is with the blonde wig? I feel very puzzled. I find out many years later that Dad was seen with a blonde woman while he was in Edmonton. When word got back to Mom, she started wearing the blonde wig to counter the rumours of Dad running around with a "blonde floozy." I'm not sure that Mom becoming blonde stopped the rumours.

What is it like for her to have a husband like Mike, who seems to have no limits on behaviour, whether it's working, gambling, eating, or drinking? Mom is left alone to care for her ever-growing family, since Mike's worldly pursuits demand his full attention. Despite the cruelties and violations in the marriage, Valentine chooses to stay with her husband, because—according to the wisdom of the day —"you make your bed, you lie in it." There is no support from the Catholic priest or her father to leave this relationship. Valentine married Mike when she was seventeen; a short while after her mother died.

*   *   *

My memories are adding pieces to the puzzle of my mother, building empathy for why she was so quick to flash into hostility. I've unconsciously absorbed some of Valentine's behaviours, and on this walk I've become painfully aware of our similarities. My relationship with resentment connects me with Mom. The smallest hint of intended insult results in a cascade of body responses that I call resentment, a sensation of flames in my gut, tension in my jaw, and a quick reaction with mean words when greeted by the party at fault. One small example? Rod starts out walking fast for at least the first part of the day, too quick for my preferred morning pace. I begin constructing stories that he walks fast because he wants to get away from me; that he has a strong need to distance himself from me because I'm undesirable as a partner and a lousy travelling companion. So as Rod and Russell typically blast off onto the trail together, I get some morning time alone to piss and moan to myself about my miserable little pilgrim life, jaw clenched, facial muscles tight, shoulders held high in my typical defensive posture.

My brain is only too happy to feed my sense of injury, with thoughts like: *He doesn't even care about me. It doesn't matter what I'm thinking or how I'm feeling, he just wants to get away from me. Why did we bother doing this walk together anyway? Nothing I say interests him, he just gets mad when I try to tell him some of the stuff that goes on in my head. I'm so tired of this way we do things together, but don't really say much to each other about what's going on.*

I'm creating stories that cause me to suffer. There may even be kernels of truth in there, but really!? And this pattern is common on what I would call a "good day." If my day is not going well, my thinking spirals into a place of wondering whether or not I will stay in the same *refugio* as Rod and Russell. In effect, I'd be doing them a favour since I am such an undesirable anyway. Rod has told me—more than once—that I take things to extremes. He might be on to something. My

husband is walking out the door first thing in the
morning, moving at his own pace, probably still waking
up, and by the end of half an hour, I'm thinking about
staying somewhere else that night. Do you think he
might be a bit confused about what's going on?

I'm doing my best to shift from resentment to
something else, anything else, and that means changing
my self-talk. I catch myself thinking things like, *He's so
insensitive* or *What a jerk, I can't believe how he ignored
me*; negative thoughts about Rod endlessly looping
through my brain. Now that I have no other distractions,
I am putting into practice some of the precepts I have
learned from the mindfulness training I've done. I step
back from my habitual defensive responses, and allow
myself to be curious about my husband's behaviour.
*What is the purpose of Rod's delayed response when I
tell him I need to eat on the trail?* If I'm feeling strong
enough, I sometimes ask him directly: "Are you
deliberately ignoring me? Or do you have somewhere
specific in mind for a stopping place?" Maybe I don't
have to take everything Rod says or does so personally.
That would give both of us more room to express
ourselves without fear of recrimination or retaliation.

Before it's time for lunch we drop down into the
town of Trabalenos, where the trail meanders beside
what the guidebook describes as "an old highway, not
used much." We end up trudging six kilometres along a
very busy transport truck route complete with roaring
truck engines, the smell of diesel fuel in the air, and litter
in the ditches. That is the "yang" of the day, made more
challenging because we can't find a quiet place to eat
our picnic lunch. I'm still having difficulty calling up
words to describe what I'm feeling to my travelling
companions so, once again, on today's lunch break I pull
out *Sailing Alone Around the Room* from my pack. I
need to hear my own voice, to ground myself in the here
and the now. The pages fall open at the poem entitled

"Idiomatic" and I begin to speak without struggling to find words, grateful that they are recorded on a page for me.

"It's a big question to pose so early in the morning ..."

Perhaps my decision to bring poetry along on this walking journey was foreshadowing the difficulty I'm having now, saying what is in my own heart and mind. It's so much easier when I pull out the book, open to a poem, and give myself permission to read aloud. It's an expression of me and not me.

Until I started listening to *The Road Home* again, I had forgotten how much I enjoy hearing poetry. Many years ago I used to write poems, but stopped when I scared myself with my honesty. Stifling my writing hand is one of the many ways I have silenced myself. Today, hearing my voice gives me more confidence, brings me back to where I am in time and space after all those hours of allowing my imagination to roam unleashed.

As I read from Billy Collins on the trail, the words in his poems seem to expand as everything around me slows down. The imagery expands in the spaces, like dehydrated vegetables reconstituting in water, becoming their full, recognizable selves again. And yet not the same as before. I'm able to feel the weight of each word, the condensed language of poetry heavy with meaning. It's possible that through this process of reading aloud I may be starting to reconstitute myself.

When I write my blog, or send emails to Emma, I can easily find words. Sitting at the keyboard, the words flow from my mind directly to my fingers without hesitation. Writing in my journal feels effortless. I just let the words drop onto the page through my pen. There's something different about talking, about giving voice to my thoughts. When I write poetry inspired by this time on the trail, I thoughtfully compress my observations into condensed language, using only what is essential.

CAMINO MEDITATION

Lift heel, leg forward,
Step into now
Arm swing, pole plant,
Breathe out

                    Ground level carpet
                        Indigo splash

Lift heel, leg forward,
Step into future
Arm swing, pole plant,
Breathe in

                Distant mountains beckon
                        Snowy heights

Lift heel, leg forward,
Step into past
Arm swing, pole plant,
Breathe out

                    Ancient hurts alive
                        Releasing

Lift heel, leg forward,
Step into moment
Arm swing, pole plant,
Breathe in

                    Curiosity guides
                Compassion transforms

My mind is occupied by poetry until we end up at Vega

de Valcarce and the *Albergue de Brasil*. This *albergue* has beds for forty-six people, a great outdoor patio area for hanging out, and a bar. People sit outside visiting with each other, sipping at tall bottles of cold beer or chilled glasses of white wine. In another area set off to the side, pilgrims are reading, creating a solitary space away from the noisy chattering crowd. The patio is our dining room. The *albergue* is not full; tonight there will be twenty-six people eating together around the large stone table. Shrubs and flowers surround the patio area, and a large sign above reads, "Camelot" to complete the fairy-tale setting.

I feel like I suddenly have too many choices. What do I do first? Have a beer? Wash my clothes? Write in my journal? Nap? After I pull off my boots and throw my pack on my bunk bed for the night, I take out my journal and head outside, finding a chair where I can sit and record my thoughts for the day. There's no Internet café here, so I content myself with an older form of writing. It's a challenge to remember the words I was putting together in my mind this afternoon. Where do those ephemeral poems sneak off to? And why do they scurry away when I have a pen and paper to hand? Rather than have a snack while I write, I order a cold beer from the bar. In the middle of scratching my words on the page, I hear Rod come downstairs from the shower and order his second beer. He has fully adapted to the pilgrim way of life.

Once I'm done my journal writing, I shower and wash out my clothes so they can dry in the remaining afternoon sun. We continue to avoid using the washing machines in the *albergues*. Washing things by hand is free and far more reliable.

I look forward to the pilgrim meal served here, since I expect it will give me a chance to get to know some of our fellow travellers, in a way that we don't otherwise as we pass each other on the trail or spy each other in a restaurant. A bell rings to call us to the table. Then the *hospitalero* introduces herself, "I am from Brazil, and I have been *hospitalero* at this *albergue* for eight years. Every year I come here for three months to serve pilgrims like you. It is important to me, to give you a good experience as you walk. I cook all the meals with love." I can feel her love as she speaks. Tears well up in my eyes, as I listen to her words and take in her tall, unshakeable presence. She follows her introduction with a prayer in Portuguese, her native language, blessing us and the food. Our meal commences.

The first course is a marinated kale salad with fresh spring greens and roasted sunflower seeds added as a garnish. Our *hospitalera* also brings out some cheese buns that are still warm from the oven. I'm thinking, *Oh my God, have I died and gone to heaven?* This food is too good to feel guilty about what I'm consuming. We clear off our plates, the signal for the next round to come out.

The second course is a Brazilian black bean stew with pork sausages, served on a bed of white rice, with flavours I've not tasted before and can't identify but find delicious. As our host clears away the dishes from our second course she announces, "For the dessert, I have made a Brazilian carrot cake with a chocolate topping. This is not like your American carrot cakes. It's much lighter, and the carrots have been grated very fine. You'll see." She delivers a light and fluffy cake that is moist and ever-so-tasty. I don't even leave crumbs on my plate.

While the meal is outstanding, the conversations I hoped for don't materialize. Most everyone else at the table is German, the predominant language spoken during dinner. We are a threesome within the larger crowd, excluded from the boisterous laughter and sharing of stories.

Rather than linger around the table after our supper meal is over, we hike up to the *Castillo del Sarracin*, perched on the hill above the town. The name makes this sound more grand than it is; it had once belonged to the Marquesas de Villafranca but it is a ruin now. It's such a relief for me to be walking again. As we climb, we are rewarded with vistas of the valley below. When we arrive at the ruins, the sun is starting to drop towards the horizon, and the light is changing into the soft oranges and purples that signal the coming of sunset. The stone remnants suggest some of the grandeur of the original Castillo. Russell and I clamber to the top of the highest hill we can find, Rod hanging back. The outlines of far away mountains beckon. At times I have to pinch myself to remember that we are in Spain. As the sun drops further, we force ourselves to head back down. We laugh together at having entertained ourselves, yet again, with more walking. We stop several times to take in the shifting light and sunset colours as we make our way back to the *albergue*.

CHAPTER 21

MAY 6, DAY 18
VEGA DE VALCARCE TO ALTO DO POIO
(21 KM)

We are blessed with another day of remarkably sunny and warm weather. I believe this is more of Saint Anthony's work. He is taking good care of us as we climb into the high country with all its magnificent vistas. Our guidebook states that we can expect rain and fog at least one day out of three. Our second day of walking in the high country is so clear we can see fields of flowers and grazing animals in the landscape below, while off in the distance are more snow-covered mountains. I had not anticipated that I would be walking into mountain ranges once we were past the Pyrenees. I feel completely invigorated by the high places. However, when the route drops down into the lower valleys and continues to parallel busy roadways this feeling dissipates.

What grabs my attention in the valleys? Lately it's been the signs adorning run-down and abandoned places for sale. The real-estate agents must see pilgrims as a possible target market. Signs in English read:

Your Galician Palace.

This Could Be Your Dream Home.

Peace And Tranquility Are Yours Here.

I suggest to Rod and Russell that one of our friends, who's always looking for a good deal on real estate, might want to check out Galician real-estate listings.

Russell comments, "Do you think he'd want to buy a broke-down palace?"

I respond, "Well if it's cheap enough, maybe. We'll have to send him some photos and see what he says."

In contrast to the untended, broken down buildings, I also see old stone homes that have been renovated to perfection. What does it take to restore a home that may be several hundred years old? This is a thought I keep to myself; it's a rhetorical question. I'd rather not hear all the details. Instead I admire the wisteria that adorns the rooftops of these homes, the purple blossoms attractive against the grey stone.

After walking through the village of Laguna de Castilla, which only has a few houses and no services for pilgrims, we spot a new style of trail marker. The stylized yellow scallop shell now displays the name of the town or village we are in, and how many kilometres we have left to go until we reach Santiago. I'm wondering why the markers have changed, when we come upon a large marker stone stating "Galicia." We have left the province of Léon, and entered Galicia, one kilometre outside of Laguna de Castilla.

After which begins another long climb. We arrive at the hamlet of O Cebreiro at noon. It is a glorious sunny day, not too hot, and we have lots of energy to keep going. Before we do, we have lunch at an inviting landscaped picnic area complete with tables and flower beds, away from the parking lot where tour buses stop and disgorge passengers. Rod and Russell check out the market while I take time to unlace my boots and give my feet a rest. Rod and Russell return to where I'm standing, giving me an update on what they've discovered. We're feeling celebratory so I join them to splurge on fruit that we buy from one of the vendors. My choice is Spanish "cheeries" (yes that was the sign in English), the first of the season. I so appreciate these small treats that aren't loaded with carbs. Although we could stick around for some of the scheduled tours and performances—Galician bagpipes included— we aren't inclined to linger with hordes of tourists.

We carry on once our lunch is complete. The land below us is carved up by roadways and farmland looking like green patchwork, and enough flowers blooming to colour portions of the entire scene in shades of yellow, white and lavender. Some of the nearest hillsides to the trail look like they've been used for gravel mining, with barren rocky tops above the greenery. The highest hills are in the distance, some of them with snowy white caps. Those beckon me forward until we hit Alto do Poio, the highest point of the day.

Although I'm ready to keep going on to the next *refugio*, Rod announces he's tired from the climbing. "Are you aware that we've been walking for eight hours already?"

"I know, and I still have energy."

"Well, I need to stop. I've had enough for one day."

Our bodies respond differently to the altitude gains and losses. I am feeling strong and confident in this moment, so unlike the times when I have thought *I can't take another step*. However, once Rod has spoken, I decide: It's okay to rest now; I'm probably more tired than I realize. *It's not fair to Rod to insist on pushing ahead.* Russell also agrees to stop without any fuss or pushing back.

Russell: "There are two places to choose from here. Mom and I can check to see whether there's room for us tonight."

Me: "Why don't you find a place to sit in the shade until we come back?"

My kindness muscle is getting stronger.

There are two *albergues* to choose from, but only one has space for us. It comes with the least friendly owners of an *albergue*, and also the least friendly pilgrims we have encountered yet. Perhaps the high climb and thin air has worn everyone out but the whole experience is rather grim from a social perspective. Everyone's body language is closed in, arms folded, heads down. When I try to make eye contact, a few individuals look up briefly, then furtively look aside. These pilgrims seem suspicious, unwilling to engage in conversation, so unlike others we have encountered on the trail. My mental image of this group is in black and white. It's unsettling.

Although my fellow travellers here aren't open to friendly conversation, and there is no Internet, I content myself in other ways. I find a spot outside that overlooks the beautiful valley we have just ascended, and lounge in the sun as I write in my journal. The three of us take a long time quietly watching the far-off mountains fade into shadow, until only jagged outlines remain visible, highlighted by the sinking sun. As the temperatures cool and stars begin to emerge, we head inside.

The life of a pilgrim has its moments.

CHAPTER 22

We get up just as the first rays of the sun appear on the mountains beyond and take our picnic breakfast outside, finding a seat on the hillside overlooking the valley to catch the full sunrise. Our perch is a grassy bank, in front of an open expanse where we get a full view of where we have come from, illuminated in shades of red and orange. This vista more than makes up for the disconnection from others I felt last night. It gets even better when Russell notices that the place serving coffee is open. Rod is as energized as I am.

"Who wants a coffee?" he asks, all chipper, so unlike his usual morning demeanour.

"We do!" Russell and I chime together.

Off goes Rod with Russell in tow, so they can bring back three ceramic mugs of steaming black coffee. As we sip our morning elixir, the sunrise slowly shifts into daylight. Low mist obscuring some of the nearby hills now melts under the direct rays of sun. That is our signal to return our cups to the café and finish packing up. Time to head back onto the trail leaving behind the crowd of people huddled around the coffee outlet.

The Camino route markers now appear every 500 metres, listing the village or hamlet along with the distance left to travel to Santiago. The trail has become so rural here in Galicia that there are times we are walking through active farms and barnyards. When we tramp through, or next to, sheep farms and barnyards, there are strong smells of manure. It's a clean smell somehow, not like the smell of used diapers left in a garbage bin for too long. The sound of roosters crowing is a constant through the rolling landscape, and I find myself strangely comforted by these small reminders of everyday life here. I wonder how real estate descriptions read when a farmer decides to sell property.

Farm house, barn and ten acres of pasture land for sale. Camino de Santiago runs through it. Must maintain access for pilgrims.

Does the Camino add more to the value of real estate? Do people adjoining the Camino feel the blessings of our walking? I occupy myself for quite some time with these questions.

Our first part of today's walk is jet-propelled by the coffee. As the caffeine passes through my system, I settle into trance mode. Then I see a poster stuck on a telephone pole that states: Barnacle Festival, August 18th, Finisterre. After I stop laughing out loud, Russell and I have fun with wild imaginings about what the Barnacle Festival would consist of. We end up creating the Barnacle Dance, which would be danced by many thousands of people at the festival. It's a little bit like the game of musical chairs we played as children, but in this dance no one gets eliminated. Before the dancing starts, everyone has to find something solid to hang onto with one hand. It could be a chair, a telephone pole, the shoulder of a person standing next to them. Whatever works. Then, when the musicians start to play *The Barnacle Song* (it may not yet be composed) festival goers raise their free arms, hands held high with fingers waving in the air while hanging on to their object with the other. Human arms wave high in the air, in the way barnacles feed with their feathery appendages, the "cirri," waving from their shells. When there's a pause in the music, the waving fingers and hands go down. People stay anchored to their spot as long as the musicians play *The Barnacle Song*. I imagine this as the highlight of the festival, followed by fireworks and much drinking. The dance would probably be preceded by much drinking as well. Perhaps Russell and I got too much sun yesterday, and our brains are like the scrambled eggs we were served for our supper last night.

Not too surprisingly, Rod holds back from contributing anything to this imagined scenario. He doesn't often engage in such silliness. Thank goodness for Russell and Emma in my life.

Now that my Barnacle Festival flight of fancy is over, I get out of my head and pay more attention to my surroundings. I can see that housing and architecture have changed dramatically in this part of the Camino. Our guidebook suggests that we can expect things to change even more as we approach Santiago. I notice grey slate roofs interspersed among the more common red tiles. Sometimes I see a thatched roof; these are less common. I'm also starting to see some of the storage structures called *hórreos*. They are most often built on a high stone foundation, designed to keep out critters that would otherwise eat the grain and corn stored inside. Occasionally, as we walk through a farmyard one of us will spot a large outdoor oven, characteristic of the lifestyle here in Galicia. There is not much observable wealth here, rather it seems as if people live close to the land, growing the food they need and selling the surplus. Some of the reading I've done has described Galician farming practices as less intensive and pesticide-reliant than other farming regions in Spain. As a result, there are riotous blooms of wildflowers throughout the region.

Walking in this countryside, it's hard to believe that we are a little more than 150 kilometres from the holy city. This is the most heavily travelled section of the entire Camino Frances and it's a strange juxtaposition of crowds against the backdrop of this rural, rustic area.

After twenty kilometres of moving through the hilly countryside, I am happy to see our destination in the distance. We are planning to stay tonight in a sixth century monastery, described as providing very basic pilgrim services, in the town of Samos. In keeping with the origins of the Camino, this *refugio* is *donativo*. I find the building to be a damp and gloomy place, as grey on the inside as it is on the outside. Stone walls do not retain or generate heat and there's no central heating in this building. This is one night where I'm grateful I brought along my sleeping bag. We're going to get what we pay for.

There are more surprises in store. When I go into the bathroom to relieve myself, I discover that all the pilgrims must use the same facilities. It's my first genderless bathroom on the Camino. At the entrance I almost get run over by an overweight man wearing only a white towel draped around his over-sized belly. He's singing loudly in a language I think is Italian. He seems proud of his body, flaunting himself about the small space we have to move around in between the sinks and the stalls. Given his wet hair, I assume he's just stepped out of the shower. I furtively look around and see male and female bodies in various states of dress and undress.

Seeing this man brings up unwelcome memories of the way Cé would enter our home and take over the space. His overweight body and big belly seemed to be a source of pride for him. I did my best to retreat from him, keeping as much distance as I could from his groping hands and leering eyes. This remembering is more than I can handle now. I decide to postpone my shower for another day.

I scuttle back to my upper-level bunk bed and jump into my sleeping bag, waiting for Rod and Russell to finish washing up. I discreetly watch the couple in the double bed below me, set in a large open space. He wants to cuddle, not concerned about all the people passing by. She seems more reserved, and keeps pushing his hands and lips away. I make up stories about how they met on the trail and how often they have snuck off into private places to have some intimacy. Now that my mind is on the track of sexual activity, I switch to my own desire for time with Rod with no one else around, remembering the places I've thought about having sex with him on the Camino: In the forest beside the rushing stream before we walked into Burgos; on the carpet of moss and blue flowers a few days ago; in the *refugio* run by the two Brazilian men, after we'd had the wineskin ceremony and a great meal; at the top of the vista this morning at sunrise. This ancient monastery is yet another place where I won't be able to indulge the physical desire I'm feeling right now. Are my body's needs over-riding my questions about being in this relationship? Does my body know something my mind hasn't arrived at yet?

Once Rod and Russell emerge from the showers, squeaky clean, unlike me, we still have time before the pilgrim meal is served to wander around Samos. As we cruise the streets, I spot a library. This excites me, since libraries have computers. Last night I had no access to the Internet, and I don't know when I'll next be able to post a blog or check for email messages. I hurry in, hoping there's enough time for me to play on the computer before the building closes. I'm in luck! Not only does this library have three terminals for pilgrims it also has air conditioning, a welcome bonus after a hot day on the trail. I register with the librarian, then update my blog. I love this time, writing my impressions, knowing that others far away are reading my words. After a day of walking in a country far from home, this feels like heaven.

With the time I have left, I check my email before I have to return to the monastery. The messages I receive are like finding water in a parched desert. Friends have responded with understanding and support for some of my more painful sharing about this journey, particularly related to the communication challenges I've been having with Rod.

> Hello Marie. Hang in there. You've been through tough times before, and you and Rod have such a strong bond. I believe that you'll find your way through the challenges to the love that is there between you. And if you don't, you will have examined your relationship as honestly as you can. I believe there is no growing without some pain. Perhaps that is the true nature of pilgrimage, fully experiencing that pain. Suffering is optional. Look for the truth behind the illusions. And remember, you don't have to keep living your present life as if it's the same as the past. You're so much more than that. No matter what you decide, I'm here for you. Love from D.

There's a message from Emma, too. She tells me:

> I'm feeling restless these days, like there's something more I should be doing but I don't know what. I'm working at a restaurant, but B tells me they are taking advantage of me. They are giving me split shifts, they make me stay longer than my shift should be, and I'm not getting paid any overtime. I'm getting frustrated, and I'm not sure what to do. I need the money but I don't like feeling used.

I have many things I'd like to say to Emma, but mostly I stay out of her decision making. I know that B has strong opinions, and his word carries more weight than mine these days. So I reflect back to her what I'm hearing:

It sounds like you're working a lot of hours, and not getting paid what you think is a fair wage. That's a tough position to be in. I also know that the restaurant industry expects staff to work long hours and split shifts are often part of the package. I trust you'll find a good solution to this situation. All my love, Mom.

My Internet time is up just as we have to return to the monastery for our evening meal.

After dinner we join other pilgrims for a tour of the Monastery. Our first tour guide is one of the monks, who speaks only in Spanish, and he does not seem to be interested in checking out our level of understanding. We follow him around for a while, feeling somewhat frustrated and confused until we hear an English tour guide nearby. We sidle over to the English group, and the next thing we know, we are part of a group that has been touring sites along the Camino for nine days. Their tour focuses on teaching participants about the architecture and various influences of the churches and important buildings. I think we've blended seamlessly into the tour group. Apparently not, since at the end of her talk, the tour guide acknowledges us as pilgrims. "Are you staying at the monastery?" We nod yes, smiling, and hoping for a friendly response. We get more than that. When the people in the group find out we are pilgrims, they begin to pepper us with questions.

"Where are you from?"

When we say, "Canada," they respond with oohs and aahs.

"Such a long way from home."

"Do you carry your packs on your back the whole time?"

"Yes, of course."

People shake their heads in disbelief.

I smile to myself, thinking, *We are known as the Canadian Family with the Heavy Packs.*

"Why are you walking? Why don't you just take a bus like we are?"

"Because I love walking so much."

"Are you a family?"

"Yes, we are."

That gets many broad smiles and nods in return.

Finally, the tour guide herds her flock onto the bus. I'm sure they're heading off to a nearby five-star hotel.

We return to our damp, gloomy dormitory.

Buenos noches

CHAPTER 23

We are 124 kilometres from Santiago de Compostela. Every day it seems as if there are more people walking with us. I find it stressful to be around so many more pilgrims. It's something I can't change, so I'm practising acceptance. Perhaps the change having the most impact on us is the lack of clean drinking water. We've come to expect that in front of every church in every small town there will be a public fountain with good drinking water, where we refill our water bottles. Now there are no more functioning public sources of potable water. Instead there are Coca Cola vending machines at trail junctions and the small villages. The fountains that exist either don't function or the water they dispense is drawn from a pool lined with green algae, smelly and unpleasant.

"This water isn't safe to drink," declares Rod. I trust his senses.

Adding to our stress, we no longer have the same easy access to bathroom facilities that we're used to. Up until we crossed into Galicia, whenever we have needed to use *baños* along the route, we have been free to walk into a bar and use their *servicios*. Not a problem, even if we buy nothing. However, today we encounter the double whammy of not being able to use the bathroom and not being able to fill our water bottles in a *Casa*

Rural. We are directed to go outside and use the pilgrim *fuente,* which provides a questionable quality of water. Rod loses his temper once again, and he walks off in a huff. Russell and I are left looking at each other in bewilderment. Rod doesn't say a thing to us as we watch his retreating back.

"What's up with Dad?" Russell asks me.

"I'm not sure. I hate it when he goes off like that."

"Do you think he'll wait for us?"

"I sure hope so. It would be such a drag to get separated now, when we're so close to Santiago."

"We'll figure things out. Let's start walking and see if we can meet up with him somewhere."

This man I've been married to for over twenty-five years, the one walking off in anger, is someone I don't know well. Maybe I've been moderating my behaviour in our marriage all this time, just to avoid scenes like this. There's no avoiding it now. I don't know what has triggered this episode, yet I feel like it's my fault, I've somehow done something wrong. My mind can conjure up the worst of the worst-case scenarios: *He's decided our relationship is over, just as I'm starting to lean towards staying with him. Wouldn't that be ironic? I'm not going to see him again on the trail, and I'll have to make my way into Santiago and back home on my own.*

I'm preparing myself for no resolution to whatever problem is happening right now, taking each step with a heavy heart.

After about twenty minutes of walking we see Rod sitting down on a bench further down the trail. He's cooled down enough to tell us what's going on for him.

"I feel so insulted. They won't even give us clean water to drink. And not letting us use the bathroom? That just feels wrong to me. It's like we don't matter anymore, that being a pilgrim isn't important. And it's strange, because up until now, I've felt respected."

He has put into words some of the unacknowledged

feelings I've had for the past few days. Rod keeps talking:

"I'm really upset about the commercialization of the Camino. Now we're supposed to buy our drinks from the vending machines rather than getting our water for free. It seems like a big rip-off, a way to take advantage of people like us. I refuse to buy anything from Coca Cola. I'll go thirsty before I use one of these machines."

Ironically, Rod has been waiting for us on a bench beside one of those vending machines.

Rod's observations allow me to consider how our role as pilgrims has shifted to being more about adding income to the economy. Some of the spiritual aspect of our journey is diluted by the commercialization we observe around us. It's like we are now walking wallets, and that's not aligned with who we are and who we have been on the Camino so far.

At the same time, much of the landscape on this route remains very attractive to me. The beauty of my surroundings is not diminished by the commercialization. If that's what it takes for the Camino to survive, maybe I better find a way to make peace with it all. Just like I did with the weather today. Even though it was overcast and misty this morning— and I wanted sun—I found myself merging with what I was observing. I became the fog, softly obscuring the hillsides, leaving only the peaks of the Arthurian legends, looking for the Holy Grail.

It's an ancient landscape with great power, when I screen out the vending machines.

Our *hostal* tonight feels more like someone's rural vacation home. It is privately run and a step up from the accommodation provided by *refugios* and *albergues*. It's worth the extra euros. There is a reading room with a view overlooking the lush green of the valley below. The three women attending to our needs are going above and beyond the level of service I've experienced up until now. When the owner saw that I was chilled, she immediately layered the wood and built a fire in the large stone fireplace. I enjoy my post-walking bottle of beer in front of the fire while we wait until the restaurant starts serving wine and the pilgrim meal. I keep wondering if all this walking will keep my liver clean of the alcohol I'm drinking. In this moment I feel great. If anyone were to ask I would say, "I love every facet of this pilgrimage, challenges and all."

The highlight of tonight's meal is dessert, a slice of Tarta *de Santiago*, the special almond cake baked in Galicia to serve pilgrims. My memory of the mouth-watering entree fades in the sugar haze of this delicious cake.

We continue to change our itinerary day by day, appreciating the flexibility we have with our time. We will keep trying to cover the kilometres required, while allowing for the possibility of not walking one day should we encounter bad weather. I do my best to offer suggestions, some of which are received positively while others drop like stones into a river.

CHAPTER 24

Oddly enough, I'm keeping track of days of the week. Waking up this *Sabado*—Saturday— morning I long for nothing more than to stay in bed with my journal for a couple of hours, then head over to the Internet terminal, checking my emails and updating my blog. If I had pajamas, I'd stay in them for the whole morning. Instead I get up and do the pilgrim shuffle as I organize myself for the day. Act One: Get up, prepare for walking, eat. I content myself with a breakfast of tahini and honey on a slice of multigrain bread, topped with banana slices. In my pilgrim-addled mind, this is the finest of breakfasts. Act Two: Step outside the doorway to rejoin the crowds on the trail. Act Three: Notice. A heavy fog almost completely obscures the trees a few metres away. The visibility between the trees and where I'm standing is so low everything looks as if it's in black and white. The nearest flowering shrub appears behind a veil, its large blossoms barely recognizable through the gauze of the mist.

Given the morning weather conditions, it's a good thing we're following the old stone walls on either side of the Camino. These moss-covered walls mark farm boundaries, another classic feature of the trail in Galicia. It's a good way to keep pilgrims where we belong. As the day progresses to mid-morning, the fog begins to lift, revealing mist-shrouded valleys and villages named on our map. All the rain seems to have generated an explosion of growing things. The many colours and textures of green in this Galician landscape remind me of Vancouver Island.

The scenery isn't enough to distract me from my primary objective this morning. I'm stumbling down the trail, looking forward to the nearest café where I can order a *Café con Leche. Grande por favor.* When we do find my morning jet fuel, I get served a truly *grande* cup of coffee with milk, the largest I've had in Spain.

The caffeine keeps me going for another 10.5 kilometres of walking, until we reach the town of Portomarin, set on a hillside overlooking the *Emblalse de Belesar,* the Belesar reservoir. I haven't felt such unsettled energy in a town since we were in Zubiri. When I check the guidebook I read that Portomarin was built up over several centuries along the Rio Miño. During the 1950s and 60s, General Franco's regime proceeded to build a dam on the river to generate hydro-electric power, which resulted in the town being relocated to higher ground. Its hillside perch suggests that it is about to take flight, wanting to land in the valley below where it belongs. I have a fleeting image of Portomarin as a modern-day Atlantis, completely submerged, with new forms of life living below the surface.

Saturday happens to be market day here, and we get distracted by the vendor displays. We leave the trail marked by scallop-shell symbols, choosing instead to meander along tables of food, clothing, and hardware displays stretching out along several streets. Given that we're arriving shortly after noon, our first priority is food.

We find a friendly cheese vendor who is happy to serve our pilgrim trio. Conducting this exchange in Spanish, Rod asks for "a taste of the sheep's milk *manchego*, please."

It's very yummy, but there's a lot more cheese to test before we make our decision.

After letting us try several other varieties, we finally make our choice. "I like this spreadable goat cheese," states Rod.

"I agree. This is so rich and so creamy," Russell enthuses.

All I can say is "Mmmmm." Our vendor gives us a special price on this locally-made goat cheese. We call him our *Ángel de Queso* - our Cheese Angel.

We walk away to a nearby viewpoint where we sit on a lawn, away from all the busy traffic, to sit and have our picnic lunch.

Before we rejoin the Camino, we take time to look at all the dry goods for sale. Racks of clothing, which I quickly paw through. Nothing appeals to me. Kitchen appliances. Don't need any of those. Chainsaw vendor. What!? In my mind, I hear the vendor calling out to passers-by: "Step right up. Get your Husqvarna here while they're still fresh." I imagine a farmer saying to his wife, "I'm going to the market to pick up a chainsaw," grabbing his wallet and heading out the door. What if the Husqvarna is intended as a gift? Do they ever come gift wrapped? What if the farmer's wife is the one doing the shopping? Is there a line of women-friendly chain-saws in our modern globalized world?

If there is, Mom could have used one. Lac La Biche didn't have a market vendor like the one in Portomarin, but Valentine still managed to use chainsaws to solve a problem at our family cottage on Beaver Lake.

* * *

"These trees are getting too big," Mom complains to Dad. "They are blocking the sun, and I hate how shady it is here now." Valentine loves to sunbathe during the summer months, one of the few times I see her in stillness. "I want you to cut down those big poplars so it's more open around the cabin and the beach."

"No way!" Dad refuses to give in. "Those trees screen us from all the boaters on the lake. If I cut them down, we'll lose our privacy."

Valentine says, "That doesn't bother me. They can stare all they want. They don't come onshore, so who cares?"

The argument goes back and forth like this for some time with no resolution. Finally, when Mike is away on one of his many business trips, Mom harnesses two of my older brothers to cut down the offending trees. An entire day is filled with the sound of chainsaws chewing through the largest poplar and birch trees along the lakeshore. Gasoline powered engines whine, volume and pitch rising until whirring teeth cut through tree trunks. I hear the cracking sound as trees topple to the ground. Then a brief pause, with the sound of chainsaw motors idling, as my brothers set up for the next cut. It is our job as the younger siblings to haul the smaller chunks of wood to the woodpile, where they will dry and season for a year. By the end of the day, we have a great stack of wood for our outdoor fireplace. Stumps and piles of sawdust along the lakeshore are all that remain of Dad's beloved trees.

When Dad next shows up at the cabin, he's outraged.

"You cut down the trees! I told you I wanted them to stay!"

Mom's response? "You want those trees? You can darn well put them back up."

This incident was so confusing. On the one hand, I admired Mom for getting her own way, without getting overruled by Dad one more time. I liked her spunkiness, even though I didn't feel comfortable with her method. I wondered if my brothers were unwilling accomplices to Mom's act of rebellion. Did they feel like they were forced to choose between one parent and another? Loyalty was an important family trait and I worried that relationships would become even more volatile. I grieved the loss of those trees, yet I didn't breathe a word to anyone. That would have been like pouring gasoline onto a blazing fire.

*   *   *

The vendors selling dry goods have tables lined up to the top of the hill by the church. At that point we discover there are no scallop shell markers to be found. After fifteen minutes of searching, we finally ask a woman exiting the church for directions. She smile and points, "It is down the hill. The Camino is not up here." Shortly after we rejoin the trail, the afternoon sun burns away the last of the low cloud. I can finally feel the heat of the sun in full force. I stop to switch out of my long-sleeve shirt into short sleeves, also adding a layer of sunscreen to my skin.

Comfort is fleeting. Within an hour, my feet begin to sing their protest song. Even though I have no blisters or broken skin, my foot muscles have still not adjusted to the constant day-to-day pounding of this long walk. I have already decided that when I arrive in Santiago, I'm leaving a load of gear there before we head off for Finisterre. No three-layer Gore-Tex jacket, I'll just carry the poncho and one pair of zip-off pants, one long-sleeve and one short-sleeve shirt, two pairs of socks (not three), two pairs of underwear (not three), one bra, and essential personal hygiene items. No pills of any kind. I'm not planning to carry the tampons or pads any further, although I've had them in my pack all this time. I stopped menstruating regularly two years ago but I still have occasional surprises.

I'll leave the warm gloves and the headband behind, too, since I have a hood on my fleece jacket and a Gore-Tex hat. I'm also going to leave the binoculars. I can't believe I've carried them this far, and used them so seldom.

We end our day at a municipal *albergue* in a place called O Hospital. Our party of three polite Canadians pauses in the entrance-way, taking time to remove our boots and put away our poles, while other pilgrims enter and immediately push past us to get to the person stamping *Credencials* and assigning beds. While we have an orderly sense of getting in line and waiting our turn, it is obvious that others don't have the same practice. My inner Buddhist has completely vanished for the time being taking with her my loving kindness and compassion. It's the end of the freaking day and I don't want to walk any further! I don't want to have to plan anything in advance, to make any reservations ahead of time. This seems to be both an advantage and a drawback.

We pilgrims are competing for scarce resources. We're like a microcosm of the state of the planet, where we all become severely competitive with each other when the supply of water, food, and a place to stay dries up. I want to stay collaborative and inclusive, and I also want a bed to sleep in at night. I suspect there will be more end of days like this one, where we have to walk further, or stay in less than stellar accommodation, because of intense demand for the limited number of beds. The closer we get to Santiago, the more pilgrims walk and bike the trail. I shudder at the thought of walking shoulder-to-shoulder with others on the way into the city.

I recall the expression "the Camino provides" and shift out of fear.

Where am I, in this present moment?

Breathe.

Notice.

I'm sitting outside, my back against the wall of the *albergue* we have secured for the night. I feel the sun on my body as I write in my journal. This hamlet is surrounded by farms. Sheep graze in an adjacent field. A solitary horse seems out of place as it munches grass along the inner fence line. One ewe comes out of a barn with two small lambs, and the entire herd runs over to greet the newcomers. Then, in sheep-like fashion, they all put their heads down and start to eat. This is my cue to head into the dormitory to grab Rod and Russell. I'm ready to put on my own feed bag.

The dining area is arranged in a series of several long tables that ensures we share our supper with other pilgrims. Tonight we must break out of our protective little bubble of three. I'm thrilled to meet a number of other English-speaking folks. Glasses of wine loosen my inhibitions and I'm able to easily strike up conversations with two people next to me.

On one side is Daniel, who tells me, "I'm from County Cork in Ireland. Look at these green fields, and all the sheep. Galicia looks just like home. I could have just stayed there and walked around the farmlands. I would have saved a lot of money." I tell him, "You've just saved me a lot of money. Now I don't need to travel to Ireland, I've just seen County Cork." His blue eyes sparkle with laughter, his whole being vibrating with aliveness. What is it with the men from the British Isles that I find so darn attractive? Dan is at least twenty years younger than I am. The Camino, the great equalizer. It's a good thing I'm traveling with Rod; I can divert my lusty thoughts and feelings in his direction.

If I could be sure we wouldn't be discovered, I'd sneak off with Rod to one of the nearby fields, hiding behind the hay piles so we could have intimate time together. I don't care how impractical the thought is; my desire has a life all of its own. I feel a rush of heat flood into my pelvis and my face turns red just thinking about the possibilities. I briefly lose focus on my companions, then quickly turn my attention to the person across from me.

Marguerite is from Sweden, tall, athletic-looking, and blonde. She's the first pilgrim I've met who has a yoga mat strapped to her tiny backpack. Before I can make too many judgments about her—I'm actually jealous of her beauty and her apparent physical well-being—she tells me, "When I first started walking, I was feeling strong. Then I got very sick and had to stay in Ponferrada for two weeks. The doctor gave me antibiotics and that didn't seem to help at all. I was wondering if I'd be able to finish my Camino. I even phoned my boyfriend to ask him to buy me a plane ticket to come home early. He suggested I wait another day or two. Then I started to feel well enough to walk again. So here I am. Tomorrow I'm meeting up with my friend, so we can finish the walk to Santiago together."

As the evening wears on, Marguerite and I share how our walk so far has changed our ideas about ourselves.

Marguerite: "I had all my plans made, and then I wasn't sure I'd be able to finish. I've never had that happen before. I had to accept that maybe my body wasn't capable of finishing the walk."

Marie: "We ended up needing to take a bus from Burgos to Ponferrada, because I wasn't able to walk as far as I thought I could each day. I didn't plan to take a bus, and I feel a little ashamed to admit that to you."

As I hear myself describe my disappointment, I become conscious that I can still love myself for carrying on, for being present and mindful on the trail, for continuing to reflect on who I am in relationship. I'm here now, and that is what's important.

Marguerite: "Do you think this journey is changing you in any way?"

Me: "I've had a few surprises. I don't think I'll know the details until I've been home for a while. There are definitely changes I want to make from what I've been learning about myself on this walk."

We continue to share in this vein, both of us willing to be vulnerable, to open our hearts to each other, even though we are relative strangers.

Before we split up for the night, heading to our individual bunk beds, our group generates a summary of what we have learned so far:

- Flat is a relative thing when looking at the maps and elevation changes.
- Don't use the washing machines in the *albergues,* they just eat money and don't do the job.
- Don't underestimate what distances people are capable of covering even when they look like they can barely move. There's an older French pilgrim who moves stiffly around the *refugios* and looks like he's not going to be able to go the distance each day. And yet, when we show up at our next destination, there he is, sitting in the plaza having a beer. Or relaxing in the *refugio,* having arrived before us. I keep being surprised by him, and by others whose bodies are giving them trouble. I have a new level of respect for the determination behind their progress.
- Don't judge people too quickly. This is a case in point with Marguerite tonight. I was ready to dismiss her as a princess. Instead I discovered she's had her own share of difficulties, and has had to dig deep in herself to carry on her journey.

Just before I fall asleep, the thought floats through my mind: *As I am learning not to underestimate others, I'm also learning not to underestimate Marie.*

CHAPTER 25

MAY 10, DAY 22
O HOSPITAL TO O COTO
(22 KM)
MOTHER'S DAY

We are walking in a surprising blue-sky morning. Sheep grazing in the fields are bathed in sunlight. No horses in sight. Everything is a lush green: the grass, leaves on the trees, and tall shrubs lining the trail. Weathered farm buildings dot the landscape as we make our way to the edge of this small village. We have left the *albergue* earlier than usual so that we can beat the heat of the midday. Now I occupy myself with mental calculations as I take each step. The Atlantic Ocean and our final destination of Finisterre is now only about 170 kilometres away. The distance to Santiago de Compostela is less than eighty-five kilometres, so we've estimated it will take us four days to get there at the rate we are walking. Then another four days to get to Finisterre, eighty-eight kilometres beyond Santiago. It's too early to torture myself with the more immediate numbers, like how far I have to walk to the next lunch stop. How many footsteps have I taken this hour? How many times have I started counting, and then gotten lost in a daydream or a memory? I have no idea how many steps I take in one hour. And really, I don't care that much, I just like the soothing sound of counting off numbers in my head when I've run out of thoughts to think. A day-time trance option, like counting sheep to fall asleep at night.

We take our mid-morning rest-and-refuel stop on the trail, sharing the chunks of thick, dark chocolate I picked up in Portomarin. We resume our steady pace along ancient stone walls that delineate the route. Another two hours, then a lunch break sitting in a small grove of trees. It's our usual cheese, meat, and bread with fruit. Soon afterwards we stop for a break at a bar in Palais de Rei. I can't resist a slice of *Tarta de Santiago*, that Galician almond cake I love so much. It's Mother's Day, a great reason to indulge.

Finally we reach O Coto. If there is a town or village here, I don't see it. However there is the Casa de los Somoza, a *Turismo Rural*, and it has room for us. Everything we need is right here. It's pricey, but Rod and Russell agree to splurge—it's my Mother's Day present. This place has an outdoor plaza with a large awning that shelters patrons from rain and sun. In our usual pilgrim fashion, we head to our room, take off our packs, and take turns in our private bathroom. This one has a full bathtub, which I jump into first. Mother's Day privileges. My desire for a swim is soothed by fully immersing my body in the hot water. Ahhhh!

As the water caresses my naked body, I start to fantasize about the "S word." I have only been able to imagine having sex to this point in our journey. I am hungry for Rod's hands on my body, wanting more than the memory of my skin responding to his caresses. I remember the sensation of his fingers gently brushing my skin, kindling my desire, heat concentrating in my pelvis. In my mind's eye I picture Rod's hands lingering on my breasts, his tongue licking my throat, slowly making his way down my belly to the sweet spot where I respond with great enthusiasm to his touch.

Enough of that! Things are just getting too hot in here!

I towel off, still enjoying all those skin sensations, and head outside to join Rod and Russell on the plaza, where we order cold beer and visit with others who are sitting at nearby tables. Our clothing, weather-worn faces, and body language tell the stories of walkers on the Camino. Our desire to eat so early also identifies us as pilgrims. No self-respecting Spaniard goes out to eat until after nine o'clock. I quickly spot the two women from England I met last night sitting at the adjacent table. We continue our conversation as if there was no interruption.

Woman 1: "We are away for two weeks."

Woman 2: "Yes, we're away for two weeks."

Woman 1: "Oh, we had to do a lot of cooking before we left."

Woman 2: "So much cooking. My freezer is full, and so is hers."

Woman 1: "The freezers are full so our husbands will have suppers while we are on this holiday."

I chuckle to myself. There's something about how they speak that reminds me of Monty Python. Perhaps it's the higher pitched voices, but more likely it's the way they echo each other.

In my mind, I think, *Hey ladies, your husbands are adults. They can take care of themselves. Why don't you tell them to grow up?*

This is exactly the kind of caregiving that I want to stop in my relationship with Rod. I think about Rod's perspective for a moment. Why would he want me to change? It must be nice to have someone attentive to your needs, trying their best to cook food you like, keep you comfortable at home, bring you coffee and tea. Does being attended to ever feel like a burden to him? He does cook and shop and make tea for me sometimes. In fact he's been very involved in helping to run our household. It's not all one-way, although I think looking after the daily routine in the house is expected of me. When Rod helps at home, I give him extra points for his thoughtfulness. When he goes to work every day at a job he doesn't like very much, is he doing that out of obligation? Would he love to say, "Take this job and shove it," and create a different kind of life for himself without the role of provider hanging over his head?

How binding are these roles we've been assigned? Who has more freedom?

As we talk, the sky gets darker and we hear the sound of thunder in the distance. Clouds keep building until, finally, the downpour begins. It's the heaviest rain we've experienced since we started walking the Camino so we retire to our room until dinner service is available. We won't have to leave the building for our evening meal, since this Casa includes a highly-recommended restaurant. As we wait for opening time, I'm at a loss for how to occupy myself. There isn't anywhere to walk, no sites of interest nearby to explore, especially with the rain pouring down. I've finished all the English reading materials I brought with me or have found along the way. Pilgrims pick up and leave books behind at each *refugio*. If only I could read German, Portuguese, or French.

I start prowling the rest of this building searching for electronic diversion. When I ask the woman at the front desk about Internet, she hands me two Spanish magazines to read instead, both of which are the equivalent of *People* magazine. They are quite entertaining, since the language is simple, and I can understand the written words with the aid of Rod´s Spanish-English dictionary. I've started to record new words I want to remember in my journal, as a way to enhance memory. Memory is a curious thing. Sometimes it remembers what I'd like to forget. Other times, I can't hold on to what I want to remember.

Given that it's Mother's Day, I reach back in time to when I became a mother. I'm so grateful for the arrival of both my children and the changes I've made in order to be the kind of parent they need me to be. Russell was born in June. Rod was teaching at that time so we had the whole summer break to learn how to parent this new being. It was a time of shared wonder and joy, the two of us focused on our baby boy.

*   *   *

We have packed up our four-person tent and our truck with supplies for two weeks, and off we go to campsites we want to explore. We have a canoe tied on to the roof rack and we are set for adventures. Russell is five weeks old. It's amazing to see the world through the eyes of our child who has just arrived on the planet. I want him to see nothing but beauty, to be surrounded by nature, to experience the places that give us joy. For this summer, we spend time by lakes with sandy beaches, where I can swim and lie in the sun while Russell sleeps in a basket nearby, shaded by a tree or large shrub. We take him out in the canoe, so concerned for his safety that we never go out deeper than a paddle depth from the shore. He sits in his car seat at the bottom of the canoe with a lifejacket strapped around the entire rig. My perspective on adventure has changed completely. Having a child is definitely the biggest adventure I have ever embarked on.

I'm probably going to be a lousy parent. I've never looked after newborn babies before. What if I end up hurting my child?

Those are fears I kept locked up inside.

By the time Emma arrives on the scene, I feel more confident about taking the kids out on my own. Even when Rod is away on archaeological field work much of the summer time—he is no longer teaching—I take Russell and Emma out to nearby parks along the Bow and Elbow Rivers. The Bow River is the larger of the two, with fierce currents in the spring fed by the snow melt from the Rocky Mountains upstream. The Elbow is calmer, running through Calgary as well, joining the Bow near Fort Calgary. There are parks along the rivers where I restore my reserves of mothering energy. I receive nourishment from Mother Earth in full measure.

*   *   *

I still do.

The stone work and ceramic tiles throughout this *Casa Rural* are attractive and inviting. As is the restaurant menu. It's a night for continued indulgence, so I order barbecued lamb chops with rice and roasted vegetables. Rod orders lamb shank and Russell orders pork medallions. Our carnivorous spirits are uplifted. Once we place our orders, a basket of freshly baked bread—still warm!— and a dish of butter is delivered to our table. Now I am in heaven. We don't often get butter for our bread. Then the house wine is poured, our constant accompaniment to every dinner. I'm not a wine connoisseur, so I have no idea what I'm drinking. We sip our pre-meal elixir, laughing about our day.

Russell asks, "Have you noticed how the British women talk like they are part of a Monty Python sketch?" At which point I burst out laughing and reply in my best high-pitched imitation of one of the characters. "Well I never!"

I get more serious as we progress through our meal. I'm gathering my courage to tell Rod how much I appreciate our decision to stay in such a beautiful place tonight. One appreciative thought leads to another, until I finally say out loud what I've been thinking about for the past few days. "As we've have been travelling together, I've been challenged to work things out rather than run away. I appreciate how, even when things are difficult, we hang in for each other and make sure there's a resolution to the problem. This is so different from what I experienced as a child. This trip is teaching me about trust and about support. Thank you."

And to Russell. "You are such a thoughtful and funny travel companion. You've helped me to believe in myself, to listen to my intuition, and to bridge some of the communication gaps that have existed between Rod and me on this trip. I couldn't wish for better travelling companions."

Best Mother's Day ever!

CHAPTER 26

MAY 11, DAY 23
O COTO TO ARZÚA
(ANYWHERE BETWEEN 20 AND 23 KM)

Plan for the day: Walk, walk, and walk some more!

We've lost our sun this morning to a soft mist coating all the hills. The air absorbs humidity as we get closer to the ocean, reminding me of home. At the same time, there are large palm trees and huge agave plants that line the trail, which I'd never see on Vancouver Island. As I walk, I imagine a tequila still somewhere on the back forty of a Galician farm, distilling a strong brew from a harvest of agave.

It's not only the plants that are larger. I point out a creature on the trail and say, "I've never seen slugs this big."

Russell says, "Some of them are large enough to eat small snakes."

Later, Russell adds, "I've been thinking about making a documentary about snake-eating slugs."

That makes me laugh. And then we're off on another flight of fantasy as we walk along side by side for a time. Laughter punctuates our footsteps.

We keep leapfrogging with the two British women, who are also on their way to Santiago. Just as we're leaving a café, they enter to have their break. As we finish our lunch break, they approach the same spot to sit down and rest. Each time we meet, it's a quick exchange of "hello" or "*Buen Camino,*" and we're off again. I can hear their laughter and it lifts my heart.

Although there are brief periods of rain, the walking remains enjoyable. With cooler weather and the relatively flat gradient of the trail, we cover the twenty or so kilometres for the day faster than usual. When we arrive in Arzúa we have our choice of several *albergues*, all within one block of each other. Another rain squall helps us to decide—we seek shelter in the closest one. We enter a newer *albergue* which happens to have a good Internet connection. I am eager to post another blog, reply to comments from friends, and check my emails. Rod and Russell can take or leave the computer connection. My digital conversations feel like a lifeline, where I have complete freedom to express my emotions without fear of censure, where I can describe my inner world in a way that doesn't come easily when I speak.

The latest email from Emma makes me smile. She's been following my blog and writes:

> Dear Mom, when I read the description of the Barnacle Dance, I laughed out loud. I could picture it all, with even more details than what you wrote about. The band playing the music is Spanish gypsy style music with a very fast tempo, and the festival goers are all wearing white costumes. People have to put on gloves with coloured ribbons hanging from each of the fingers, to look like the feeding tentacles that barnacles use.

I love how she really gets my sense of humour. I write back:

> Dear Emma, Yesterday I had the best Mother's Day ever. The only thing missing was you, but I still felt your presence. As I walked yesterday, I was remembering the day you were born, how you were in such a

hurry to arrive. Rod and I had just finished serving supper to our guests when my water broke. It was all so civilized, in an unusual way. We left Russell in the care of our good friends, while Rod helped me into the car and took off for the hospital, trying hard not to break any traffic laws. My contractions were strong, and their spacing was speeding up as we were driving. Once I got to the hospital, the nurses started orienting me to the delivery room. That's when you decided to show up. The doctor on duty had to run to be there in time for your arrival. Shortly afterwards, Rod, you, and I were together in our hospital room. I remember holding you, looking down at your dark hair, your eyes wide open, gazing at me in your beautiful perfection. Rod looked at me in wonder. "We have a baby!"

"She's an Emma," I declared. You arrived with your name. This wasn't the one we had picked out for you before you were born. You didn't get to meet Rod's mother, yet I think you are carrying some of her energy forward into this next generation: loving presence, knows who she is, connected to family and community. You are Emma, through and through.

The two British women also end up here, the third night we're sharing the same shelter. Tonight we swap more details about our homes and the lives we have left behind to walk our Camino.

Woman 1: "We live in Dorset. That area is also called the Jurassic Coast."

Woman 2: "We share a second home in Portugal. We often go there with our husbands, all four of us together."

Woman 1: "This is our time. We try to do something

on our own every year. This is the longest we'll have been away."

I am struck by their joyful faces, traveling unencumbered, not looking after others. And yet:

Woman 2: "Even though I love this, I'm looking forward to getting home."

Woman 1: "I hope they're eating well while we're gone."

I imagine the men going to the pub each night, and the women returning home to freezers full of the food they prepared before they left. I'm pleased to meet a few people in this *albergue* that I didn't think I would see again. I say hello to Marguerite from Sweden, still carrying her yoga mat, still strong, making her way to Santiago. She introduces me to her friend Trevor. I ask, "How is your Camino?" His wide smile says it all. I recognize a young man from Austria who we met when we were taking the bus from León to Ponferrada. I had first noticed his tiny backpack, and wondered whether he was carrying any extra clothing. I check in with him. He reports, "I got very cold with the rain, so I had to buy a jacket. I tried to walk too far the first four days, and I started to feel very sore. I didn't know if I'd be able to continue. Now I'm doing less distance." He shrugs his shoulders somewhat nonchalantly. "I didn't know what to expect."

Two more sleeps until we walk into Santiago. I wonder which of my fellow pilgrims will arrive at the same time we do. And I'm curious about those snake-eating slugs—are they heading toward the Cathedral as well?

CHAPTER 27

MAY 12, DAY 24
ARZÚA TO ARCA-PEDROUZO
(20 KM)

I am grateful we had the clear sunny days for our high walk and climb through the Cantabrica Mountains. Today we are experiencing the true Galician climate, rainy interludes with occasional glimpses of sun. Many of the locals walk around in rubber boots, just as we do in Courtenay during the winter. In fact, there's a lot about this area that continues to remind me of Courtenay.

Thinking about home sparks thoughts about Emma and whatever she might be doing right now. I'm recalling my recent Mother's Day on the trail and Russell's generosity. I feel so loved by each of my children, in their own special ways. There were times when I did not feel I had love to give to them when they were young and needing so much of my care and attention. When Emma was crying with colic for hours on end, day after day, for many weeks, I could feel myself fill with frustration. *I would like nothing better than to just fling this baby against the wall and get her to shut up! I am so sick of walking around and holding her, the only thing that seems to calm her down. And she needs to nurse so much. How can such a small being eat so much? I feel like an over-used cow.* And yet in spite of whatever exhaustion, tiredness, pain, and frustration I may have been feeling, I still found pools of love and patience inside of me I didn't know existed.

This baby deserves to be loved. She needs to hear me say I love her, even when she's been crying for hours. I want her to know that she's loved.

I dug deep to find my mothering self. The digging sometimes led to painful memories, which needed to be unravelled during intense healing work. Moments with my adult children, appreciating each other, make it all worthwhile. Walking with Russell, learning more about who he is and the values he stands for, have made this trip extra special for me. Together, Rod and I have raised a respectful young man. He is also transforming the energy of the past. Russell and I share the same sense of humour, and his mind his mind follows mine easily into the realm of imagination. Sometimes Russell says something that is in my mind before I open my mouth. "Get out of my head," I tease.

We walk alongside large garden plots that are being planted with a variety of vegetables. I marvel at last year's remnants of kale stalks that are much taller than I am. It's a new experience to walk beside a kale forest.

Arca-Pedrouzo is one night away from Santiago. We settle into the Municipal *refugio* with tightly-spaced beds and a unisex shower area with open stalls. When I first look into the bathroom, I see a tall man with a flat belly and muscular chest preening at the mirror, a skimpy towel wrapped around his hips. Please, not again! To clinch my decision to shower or not to shower, a turn of the tap reveals only cold water. No shower for me tonight. I don't care that I'll have to go two nights without one. I've reached the limit of what I will tolerate.

As I stow away my boots and hiking poles for the night, in the cubbies and boxes set up at the entrance for this purpose, I notice a group of about a dozen young people enter the building carrying six-packs of beer and bottles of wine, laughing and singing, loudly calling out to one another. A party atmosphere is in the air and it's only late afternoon. This does not bode well for tonight.

I am hopeful they are staying in a different wing of this very large dormitory.

Now that I'm so near to Santiago, I'm thinking more about what awaits me when I return home. I find myself fussing, sometimes in my mind, sometimes out loud.

"I wonder if there will be any work for me when I get back," I say to the guys. Because I work on a contract basis, I always feel a sense of uncertainty. "I've been spending more money than I expected on this trip. I'm already worried about having to pay off my credit card once I'm home."

Russell looks at me and says, "I don't understand how you can be worried. You always talk about how there's more work than people to do it. Why do you think things will change so quickly in a few weeks?"

Good question. Could it be that there's still a part of me that feels disposable? That when I'm not in the office, not physically present to remind people that I contribute to the team, the management leader will forget about me, or won't want to use my skills anymore? I am reluctant to voice these thoughts aloud.

I respond to Russell's query: "It's probably connected to some part of my early history. I don't always know why I think the way I do, or why I'm so afraid of losing my ability to earn money. It's always there."

"I know, and it bothers me, because it's not what I see happening. I wish you'd stop worrying so much."

Rod chimes in, "You are very skilled at your work, and your colleagues know that. I think that as long as the company has ongoing projects, you will be kept busy."

"Thanks guys. I'll do my best to believe that I'll have work when I get home. It takes a lot of energy to worry as much as I do."

As I continue walking, I'm doing my best to believe in a generous, abundant universe. I know "the Camino provides," since I've experienced the generosity of others, including from my travel companions, so many times. So why not translate what is happening on the Camino into the rest of my life? Like the way I've been focusing on appreciation whenever I catch myself thinking negative thoughts. I discovered early on just how unproductive it is to spend my whole day focusing on nothing but the irritating traits of the person walking next to me. Holding on to resentment doesn't help me make the deeper connections I long for. I've shifted from thinking it might be time for me to end my relationship with my husband to revisiting our shared history, the values we hold as individuals and as a couple. My increasing physical desire for my husband is like a barometer for the changes going on inside.

On a trip like this over such a length of time, I'm getting a better understanding of the inner workings of the man I'm married to. I am more conscious of how Rod's behaviours are connected to his denial of self. He doesn't use "I" language easily, and still has a tendency to speak about his own experience in the third person.

"People usually want to walk into Santiago by the early afternoon."

"It's common for pilgrims to have a celebration after they've finished their walk."

"People get tired as they approach Santiago."

While these statements may be true as generalities, I'm not content to let Rod express himself in the third person so I've been asking him:

"How do *you* feel?"

"What would *you* like?"

"What do *you* think?"

He's responding to this new challenge I've presented to him. It's a new realm of growing for both of us as he finds his way to "I." Rod catches himself as he practices this new form of communication:

"Do you want to.... I would like to stop here for a break."

"People think ... I think that paying ten euros to enter a cathedral is too expensive."

I am also bringing my behaviours in this relationship

to consciousness. I maintain a high level of vigilance in our interactions, anticipating Rod's needs before he says anything out loud. For example, when we were staying at the pension in Burgos, I made sure to move the furniture back to all their original locations, because I notice how much it bothers him to have things out of order when we leave a place. It's one of the many silent ways of showing him how much I care. On a deeper level, I may be making choices as if I'm still in my family of origin, trying to avoid any harsh judgment for not doing things "right." Do I need to feel so responsible and be so attentive with my adult partner? How much does my hyper-vigilance get in the way of more honest interaction? This slowing down of our give and take is allowing me to examine more deeply how I am showing up. If I look back on the first day in Saint Jean, when Rod bought two loaves of bread, I recall how I rejected his generosity. And yet here I am hovering over him, and sometimes feeling resentful about my sense of responsibility to him.

I constantly monitor subtle cues from Rod to divine what he's thinking and feeling. Reading his body language so effectively means that he doesn't need to tell me much about what's going on inside. Instead, I make choices based on his non-verbal signals and my inner radar. On the past couple of mornings it became obvious to me that Rod has not been enjoying the tahini and honey I put on the table for breakfast. He usually eats everything in front of him, focusing on the food. At the end of the meal his plate is clean except for a few crumbs of toast. Unfinished pieces of bread left on his plate signal his low enthusiasm for the toppings I provided. He didn't say anything about what he preferred when we were at the market, so I bought what I wanted. To show him that I've noticed, when we are at the market today, I suggest, "Let's find some soft cheese and marmalade for breakfast tomorrow."

"That's a great idea," Rod replies.

I'm curious about why he waits for me to take the initiative to make the change. He may have continued to silently endure food he doesn't enjoy without my suggestion. I wonder how much his parents encouraged Rod to ask for what he wants or needs.

I observe this pattern I'm describing once again, as we wander the market, looking for the perfect cheese. When his eyes land on something appealing, Rod says, "That vendor will never agree to cut smaller chunks from those big rounds in the case." I have more faith in getting what we want, since every other market we've been to has given us the quantities we ask for. For once I step forward to request in Spanish, "I would like 500 grams of the soft goat cheese, *por favor.*" The vendor nods, happy to oblige. More evidence that Rod believes he doesn't have the right to ask for what he wants. How has this trait played out in our relationship?

I continue to be curious about the nature of our bond. I know it is strong, as D pointed out in her email. Is our connection more non-verbal? Have I been looking for evidence of his loving in the wrong places? It's so much easier for me to express love openly to my women friends and to my children than it is to Rod. I feel this is a great loss. I also ask myself, what of Rod's qualities do I find attractive? What about those things that Rod says or does that honour me as a person? What are the ways he lets me know I am important? What are the ways that he responds to me that show his understanding of what I'm trying to say?

It's not necessarily in the words he says. It's more often in the things he does. His love language is *doing.*

What if I focus there?

CHAPTER 28

MAY 13, DAY 25
ARCA-PEDROUZO TO SANTIAGO
(21.5 KM)

As I slowly awake I feel Valentine's presence, the strength of her joy that I'm so close to Santiago. I can hear my astral-plane mother clapping her hands with glee, along with her Valentine-giggle that signals her unabashed support for what I'm doing. It's not a sound I heard often when she was alive. Is she waiting for more souls to be liberated from purgatory when I enter the Cathedral in Santiago? Is that what she's been hoping for? I remember saying the rosary for the souls in purgatory when I was a child. I haven't been walking for that purpose, but it's possible there's more going on with this pilgrimage than I can ever consciously know. It's an unusual feeling, to bask in my mother's approval. I lie in bed for a few more minutes filled with a sense of wonder.

Communing with Valentine leaves me feeling ungrounded as we make our way back onto the trail. A large wave of pilgrims is on the move as we leave the *refugio*, and we are soon walking within a loud, boisterous crowd making its way toward Santiago. What happened to the peaceful silence I have associated with early-morning walking? It's much harder to find the solitude I crave, the quiet that helps me find my way back to myself. It's like we've joined a noisy flock of starlings fluttering about the pathways with our bodies and backpacks, migrating, somewhat haphazardly perhaps, to our final destination.

I keep shifting between two worlds, drawn into the exuberant energy around me and yet needing to retreat inward. One minute, I'm looking forward to arriving at the finish, and the next, I'm not sure I want this trip to end. I'm anxious about the future and I've loved what I've completed so far. In a moment of complete honesty I acknowledge that I'm ambivalent about endings. It's hard to ignore the push-pull between waves of joy and loss that saps my energy.

Breathe.

Notice.

Breathe.

Instead of pulling into my silent cocoon I start a conversation with Russell, who is walking beside me. "I have such a mix of emotions and sensations going on right now. It might sound strange, but I feel as if my mother is walking beside me right now."

"That makes sense, from everything you've told me about her. She's probably happy you're about to enter Santiago."

Feeling encouraged, I continue: "I'm missing Emma. It would be wonderful to have her with us as we walk into the plaza in front of the church, to have her join us as we enter the Cathedral."

"I've been missing her too. I think she'd like to be with us for the time in Santiago."

When we catch up to Rod, I give him the thumbnail version of our conversation. I share how I feel about not having to walk every day. "On the one hand I don't want this journey to end, and on the other, I'm looking forward to this journey being over."

Rod says, "I'm feeling some of those same things. Mostly, I'm looking forward to the not-walking."

We carry on in an easy silence, matching the rhythm of our stride with the swing of our walking poles. I focus on positive thoughts. I trust Rod in many ways. I can count on him to show up when he says he will; he's great with handling money and he is not aggressive in his interactions with people on the trail. I love watching Rod engage in Spanish conversations, seeing an extroverted side of him that is not always visible at home. I wonder if he is more awake to his surroundings when we're in a new place. He has proven himself to be reliable and constant on this journey. I can no longer tell any other story about him, no matter what my pre-Camino self might have to say. In fact, I've been taking apart an old narrative, letting go of what no longer fits. The new version I'm creating for my marriage is being written with every step I take.

Signs of a large city appear several kilometres outside of Santiago. Planes occasionally take off and land from the airport. At this point in our pilgrimage it's hard to believe there is any other way to get around than by foot. We stop at *Monte do Gozo*, the spot where pilgrims used to get their first glimpse of Santiago's cathedral spires. The views from the Mount of Joy are now obscured by vegetation. Perhaps the large sculpture on the hilltop built to honour a visit by Pope John Paul II in 1993, a holy year, was intended to make up for the missing view of the cathedral.

Coincidentally, 1993 was the year I started my healing journey. Looking back, I can say that was a sacred, if painful, year for me. When I started to acknowledge the violence of my childhood I was forty, Russell was six, Emma was four. I am struck once again by the between-two-worlds theme that continues to shape my day.

Before we depart this area, we drop down the hillside to have a look at the large municipal *albergue*, also constructed in 1993. We wander through the empty building that houses 500 pilgrims, marvelling at its size and stillness. Suddenly, I grasp that noon is an in-between time for the pilgrim hostels. It's empty—even the *hospitaleros* are nowhere in sight—because travellers either have left or are still on their way to this stop. I think back to all the places we've stayed at along the way and imagine a version of this *refugio* purgatory, each building waiting for the next wave of pilgrims to occupy the space. I have no desire to spend much time here, so we carry on into the city, finding a park close to the outskirts where we sit and have our lunch. I am preparing myself for the final stage, more anxious than I was this morning now that we are within the city limits.

The walk to the Santiago Cathedral within the city limits has a familiar pattern to it. City-long blocks of multi-family housing and rows of adjoined townhomes built out of brick are broken up by occasional green spaces. Public transit buses roar by, stopping frequently to take on or let off passengers. I'm not tempted in any way to board one. I'm determined to walk this route, no matter how I feel or how long it takes. As I plod along I'm grateful for the well-marked yellow arrows and markers that keep us on track; with the increase in traffic and pedestrians there's much to pay attention to. Three sets of eyes help us avoid wrong turns.

The closer we get to the cathedral, the more pilgrims converge on our route until we all spill into Plaza de Obradoiro. I feel like a deer in the headlights. It's taken us more than two hours of walking to finally arrive at the enormous cobblestone square in front of the church. People are swarming around me, exchanging greetings; I hear sounds of exuberant reunions. This swirl of activity unsettles me even more. I'm almost wringing my hands by this point, telling the guys, "I can't locate the right area, this guidebook description doesn't make sense to me." Even Rod seems disoriented, as we wander back and forth along the length of the plaza looking for the entrance to the Oficina del Peregrino where we will get our *Compostela*, our certificate of completion for this portion of the walk. How can we be lost when we've already navigated many kilometres? Russell quietly says to Rod and me, "You guys are acting really weird right now." Perhaps it's the way that Rod and I are getting more short-tempered with each other. Maybe Russell has noticed that I've lost my problem-solving abilities and am slipping into panic mode.

At the moment when I'm ready to give up in frustration, I run into the British women excitedly waving their *Compostela*. With their clear instructions, we finally find the right doorway leading up to the second floor. The line-up starts at the plaza level and slowly moves up the staircase as each pilgrim gets their certificate processed. No one is coming back down the stairs, so there must be a different exit. We patiently wait, talking quietly until it's our turn to step up to the long counter. I am asked, "Did you walk for spiritual or religious reasons, or recreational?" I respond, "Spiritual." I'm surprised by my answer. I didn't start out this walk with a spiritual intention and yet it now feels true.

When Russell is asked the same question, he answers, "Recreational." When asked a second time, again he says, "Recreational." I suspect Rod's response will be the same as Russell's. Instead, without hesitation he says, "Spiritual." I look at him wide-eyed. This man has not been comfortable with conversations about spirituality since we made the decision to leave the Catholic Church. Now I'm curious. I look forward to having time and space with Rod to share the reasons for our choices.

With the paperwork completed, we go to the main entrance of the cathedral and follow some of the prescribed pilgrim rituals described in our guidebook: We touch our right hands to the middle of the central column of the Tree of Jesse, giving thanks for our safe arrival. We wind our way in a long line of pilgrims moving toward the high altar to hug the jewelled statue of Saint James. We go down into the crypt where we pay homage to the bones of the saint.

I'm going through the motions, almost in a state of shock. I'm just not connecting with these icons and I feel distressingly out of synch with everyone around me. I feel as if I'm giving false witness, because I don't believe the mythology about the arrival of the saint on the shores of northern Spain. My cynical self believes it's a story concocted by the Catholic Church to secure a stronghold in the Iberian Peninsula, the means to creating a faith community that will stand against the Moors. This pilgrimage is as political as it is sacred. While I honour the sacredness of the walk we have completed, I am also aware of the oppression, violence and destruction that has been perpetrated as a result of religious beliefs. So what am I celebrating? Who am I honouring and why? I am filled with anger and shame for thinking these thoughts. I stumble my way to the exit, bumping into a pillar as I make my way, nearly tripping on a backpack discarded on the floor.

Once we're back out in the huge plaza in front of the church, I observe groups of pilgrims, now friends, united and reuniting, hugging each other, congratulating each other, making plans to meet for dinner. We are not a part of these celebrations. It seems our trio has been too successful at keeping ourselves separate. I feel wistful, wishing I could be a part of something bigger, longing to enter into this exuberant energy. I don't have long to linger in my discomfort. Since we're leaving for Finisterre tomorrow, we have to get ready for another four days on the trail. We don't want to spend time in all this chaos. However, exiting the square we encounter a few familiar people. Marguerite, yoga mat visible on her pack, greets us with a question, "What are you doing to celebrate getting here?"

"We're leaving for Finisterre tomorrow, so we're not quite finished yet."

"You're crazy! Why would you keep walking?"

We shrug our shoulders and laugh. "Because we're Canadian."

I think to myself, *Because we are pagan rather than Christian. Because we worship Mother Earth not Jesus. Because the Atlantic Ocean means more to us than the cathedral.*

We have to keep moving to get ready for tomorrow's trek. We find a reasonably priced pension located on the route leading to Finisterre. It doesn't take long for us to wash our clothing and clean our bodies. Then it's back into the centre of Santiago, where the Camino continues to provide. We find the post office and, with no hassle at all, pick up the two boxes of excess items we mailed to ourselves from Najera on April 27.

It's easy to get carried away by the attractions displayed in the many shops that exist in this historic part of Santiago. My chocolate pilgrim guidebook-in-progress gives a five-star rating to a specialty chocolate shop where each sample melts in my mouth, leaving me wanting more. I try to make each one last as long as possible: chili-chocolate, sea salt, with nuts, coconut, espresso. There are many shapes to choose from, although I'm disappointed to report there are no chocolate apostles for sale. I keep it simple and buy four thick rectangular bars, one for every day that we will be walking to Finisterre.

I have high expectations that here in Santiago, I will find the peanut butter I've been craving. Not so. Our search yields nothing, *nada, nyet*. Spaniards are not consumers of peanut butter, for reasons I don't understand. Perhaps they prefer Nutella, a sweet chocolate-hazelnut spread sold in one kilogram containers that fills many grocery store shelves. I sigh inwardly as I accept I have four more days of eating more of the same.

Today we must also buy our tickets for the flight from Santiago to Barcelona. A travel agent familiar with the pilgrim trade efficiently handles our request. I am able to conduct most of the transaction in Spanish, which I feel proud about. In fact, I have many conversations in Spanish tonight, instead of relying on Rod like I usually do.

When hunger stalls our errand-running, we search for a place to eat. Russell craves sushi, which is nowhere to be found. If he desired octopus—*pulpo*—he could be easily satisfied since it has appeared on menus everywhere in Galicia. We find a restaurant in the heart of downtown and enjoy a meal with fresh vegetables and shellfish, sharing a stew filled with mussels, clams, and scallops. The green salad I consume satisfies me.

As we eat, I share with Rod and Russell: "This time in Santiago does not feel like the end at all. I guess that's not too surprising, since Finisterre is really the destination I've been aiming for."

Rod says, "I'm so glad we're not sticking around for any more time here. I'm ready to carry on." Russell is also anxious to get started on this final push to the ocean.

In the midst of this discussion, I'm struck by how we're not yet celebrating. Working out logistics and planning ahead has taken over any sense of accomplishment I might have felt here in Santiago. When we get to the end I wonder if we'll celebrate at all.

CHAPTER 29

MAY 14, DAY 26
SANTIAGO TO NEGREIRA
(23 KM)

My body decides to acknowledge arriving in Santiago by giving me the first menstrual period I've had in many months. It's a heavy flow. I'm grateful for having carried emergency pads in case of this exact situation. Although I had planned to ditch the feminine hygiene products here, I won't be doing that now. While I'm annoyed that my period has arrived, there's not much I can do about it, so I brace myself for a trying day. There's no question about not walking; it is not an option.

As is typical with Day One of my menstrual flow, my energy is low. My desire to cover twenty-three kilometres today is severely dampened. I don't want to go into the gory details of my physical situation with the men, especially Russell. That's not the usual sort of information a mother shares with her son. I tell Rod the snapshot version, since he has lived with my female cycles—and the mood shifts that go with them—for decades and has always been gently supportive. When we were living in Calgary, I used to track the days between menstrual flows. I could tell by how cranky I was getting, and how much chocolate I was craving, that my period was about to arrive. Yesterday, my first clue should have been my extravagant purchase of chocolate.

I tend to focus inward on Day One and today I don't

speak much. Whatever I have to say would be more about my discomfort, my low energy level, and how I wish I could just find a comfortable place to lie down. I'm missing Emma. I'd love to have her here with me now since she understands this aspect of being a female, having suffered from menstrual cramps that knock her out for two or three days a month. She inherited the heavy flows my mother experienced, and that's been a rough start to her maturation as a woman. I've read somewhere that in ancient cultures women would be sent off to a special women-only area during their bleeding time. It was a space of quiet, rest, and renewal, often in silence. Where is that space now? I'd be walking toward it in a heartbeat.

It's not just me having a rough time. Russell seems to have developed an allergy to seafood, so he was up several times in the night with diarrhea. To accommodate our low-energy bodies, we have a slow start to our day. We have freedom this morning with no *hospitaleros* hustling us out the door by eight o'clock. Instead we leave our pension and walk over to the cafe across the street. After a quick look at the menu, we order the first bacon and egg breakfast we've had in Europe. As is the constant pattern, I notice that most of the patrons in this place are men. Russell and I have been curious, asking each other, "Where do the women of Spain hang out?" When we go into bars, it's mostly men sitting around in groups of six or more, tables filled with male bodies smoking cigarettes and drinking alcohol. Are the women living secret lives while the men are away? Are there women-only bars? Is this how rural life in Spain in structured, with the women sequestered at home? Women are most visible in the plazas, mothers and grandmothers watching their children and grandchildren playing soccer, running and laughing throughout the square. Women are also visible as owners or employees in the stores and cafés we enter.

Like this café, which is run by a husband-wife team.

The man comes to take our orders and the woman cooks up our food in the kitchen. They work together to deliver our meals, she carrying two plates, he holding a carafe of coffee in one hand and a plate in the other. This couple also owns the pension we've stayed in, and we arrange to return here when we come back from Finisterre. They graciously allow us to leave a pile of excess gear with them so we can lighten our packs for this final stage of our walking journey. Back at the pension I am amazed at how much stuff we take out of our packs, most of it mine. What was I thinking, the queen of de-cluttering and travelling light? Well, to be honest, I was thinking spring in the Pyrenees with lots of variable weather conditions, wanting to be warm and dry when the weather was nasty.

I have been warm and dry, just with a heavy pack on my back.

I muse about how much harder it would be to walk if I was still carrying all that gear. Even with less weight in my pack, my body is not willing to walk far without a rest. I don't think the men can appreciate how much having a heavy menstrual flow affects my mood, my energy levels, and my ability to keep walking without a sit-down break every hour. My slow pace is frustrating to Rod, who is fired up today. Even Russell is walking faster than I am, although with less enthusiasm than usual.

Leaving Santiago, I notice that the Camino markers are more precise than usual. At the city limits, the mileage posted to Finisterre is 88.022 km. I am astounded. "Rounded to three decimal places; how did they do that? That's smaller than a toenail."

Russell does a quick calculation. "Actually, .022 kilometres equals a little more than 72 feet."

"Oh, I take it back. No creature on earth would have a toenail that big."

As we exit the city, my eyes are drawn to splashes of bright colour. Orange walls stand out against the almost lemon-yellow fields of canola, while in the background a home painted in dark yellow stands watch over the scene. The oranges, yellows, and reds of the hillsides we've walked beside are replicated here in buildings painted with the colours of Spain. It's a moment of welcome distraction from an otherwise uncomfortable effort.

Today's events seem to be nudging me to accept that it's important to let myself slow down and take care of myself, to carefully listen to the needs of my body. I have to make sure I'm walking at a pace I can sustain, speaking up, insisting on taking the breaks I need. I make it to lunchtime, grateful to find a small park with several wide benches beside a slow-moving river where I can relax in the sun. We get out our lunches in a familiar routine. Russell pulls out the salami, I've got cheese, and Rod carries the bread. We pass the items around, slicing off what we need with our pocket knives to create sandwiches on the spot. We finish up with apples that come out of Russell's pack. As our pile of food grows smaller and my tummy gets full, a short woman wearing a brown shapeless dress approaches the park, her short grey hair tightly curled around her face. She takes a seat on the bench furthest away from us. Russell and I look at each other. In a comic strip, this is where the light bulb goes on above the main character's head.

This is where the women hang out.

She stays seated, resting her neck on the back of the bench, turns her face up to the sun and closes her eyes.

"She's got the right idea," I whisper to Rod. I surreptitiously take a picture of her in repose. There is a lesson here for me.

Exactly an hour later, the woman wakes up, brushes off her dress, and leaves the park. On our next rest stop, Russell and I find another bench. We take up the woman's pose. Rod grabs his camera.

We laugh together. The next moment, I become

curious about Valentine and rest. The only place I ever saw her relax was at our cottage when she was sunbathing, and that was a rare occasion. Most of the time she was busy with the constant work of maintaining the household: cleaning, cooking, baking, sewing. She sewed many of our family's clothes and was an excellent seamstress. She spent many hours in the garden outside and also loved landscaping our large yard. Every winter she'd plan out new designs and in the spring, she insisted that the boys help her dig holes and move trees. I was always glad I was a girl then, since I wasn't interested in gardening or landscaping. It also looked like hard labour and I was even less interested in that. Mom was actively involved in organizing church bazaars and she played the organ at the weekly masses. She was the mastermind behind the feasts for large family gatherings during traditional holidays like Thanksgiving, Christmas, and Easter. Did she ever sneak off on her own to get some precious time to herself? Did she ever go snaring fish on her own? Was "going to the bush" to pick blueberries in the fall with her friend Lottie a form of rest? She probably never would have answered these questions were she still alive, and now I content myself with making best guesses while I walk.

Resuming my slug-like pace, I'm enjoying the spaciousness of travelling without the masses of people we encountered on our last few days walking into Santiago. The downside of fewer pilgrims is fewer services to support walkers. When we arrive at the *albergue* in the town of Negreira it has beds for only sixteen people. It's already full, so we search for any nearby pensions. We end up on the second floor of an old hotel. I'm happy to have a room of our own because it includes a private bathroom. An unexpected blessing. When I look out the window of our hotel room, I see a town in a state of renovation. A crane is perched atop a nearby roof and the sidewalks on the street below me are torn up. The buildings look worn and aged, a little like how I'm feeling at the moment.

While we are grateful to have a room for the night, we are concerned that for the next sixty kilometres of travel, there will be few pilgrim hostels. I've heard a rumour that the next *refugio* on the route is closed. This means sixty kilometres between where we are now and the next pilgrim accommodation. We're doing our best to find out whether the rumour is true, talking to the hotel owner and other pilgrims to find out the current situation. We are determined to finish this walk to Finisterre. The route could be circuitous and I am confident we will get there as planned.

I've been walking long enough to know, deep in my bones, that all will be well. That phrase —"the Camino provides"—surprisingly has, despite my scepticism, proven to be true throughout our journey. So rather than fussing and worrying, I'm going to channel the woman I saw on the bench today at lunchtime. I will relax and have a good rest.

CHAPTER 30

MAY 15, DAY 27
NEGREIRA TO OLVEIROA
(33 KM)

My first thought this morning is, *I have to walk thirty-three kilometres today.* Followed by an inward groan as I burrow deeper into my sleeping bag.

This attitude won't help, I think to myself. *Just put one foot in front of the other, that's the only way I'll get there.*

And up I get, following my well-developed morning routine. Then out the door with Rod and Russell, searching for breakfast and strong coffee to kick-start my day. I never drink this much coffee at home, but right now it is essential. I'll have to wean myself off caffeine when I return to Canada.

I should probably wean myself off my daily third-of-a-bottle of wine, too, but then why would I do that?

We exit Negreira through an old stone archway spanning the whole street. We quickly find ourselves on an unpaved road in a rural countryside, walking through a mix of farms and forest. Trees on the adjacent hillsides spread their springtime arms upward; fresh green-leafed branches etched against the sky. The farms we pass by display small, well-worn tractors, well-suited to the size of the mixed farms here. The size of Galician farm machinery is in sharp contrast to the big air-conditioned monsters I'm used to seeing on the Canadian prairies.

Instead of scallop shells, old tractors mark our way. Right on schedule, my feet start to ache by late morning. I anticipate that by the time I get to the last ten kilometres of this stage I will be in agony. It doesn't seem to matter how close I am to the end of this journey, I still must endure the moment-by-moment physical sensations of my feet. Over the past twenty-six days I have developed several tactics to help me stop focusing on the pain, and I need every one of them to make it to Olveiroa.

Sing the verses to whatever songs I can remember, in my head, over and over again: I start with "These Boots are Made for Walking" and do my best to embody that Nancy-Sinatra attitude I witnessed when I saw her sing that song on *The Ed Sullivan Show*. My thirteen-year-old self loved her performance.

Look up, look around, notice what's beautiful: I pay attention to what I love about this moment. Birds, flowers, and foliage direct my mind away from my feet.

Call up my favourite folk festival memories and relive them in slow motion, detail by detail: Like the time Oysterband was playing the main stage at the Salmon Arm Roots and Blues Festival, and I was dancing in the area fenced off for dancers. Memories surfacing, at unexpected times in surprising places like this, most often grip me as if they are happening again in the present moment.

*   *   *

My friend Pete almost throws me over the fence when the band walks off the stage to wander into the crowd, continuing their song without missing a beat. I run up behind the band, still dancing my folk festival dance. The lead singer catches my movements in his peripheral vision and turns around, not sure what is happening. At the same time, I see three large security volunteers converging on me. I scamper back to the dancer's side of the fence without getting caught.

*   *   *

The best part about this memory is that my dancing moment with Oysterband was captured by the festival videographer, which ended up in the promotional video for the following year's Roots and Blues Festival. My fifteen seconds of fame. Just thinking about that experience energizes me. Remembering my dancing body keeps me going.

As I walk and the pain continues, I try everything. Pretend I don't have feet. Imagine I have wings and I can fly. Focus on the pain in my right hip or my lower back to take my mind off my feet. Surprisingly, that helps.

Sometimes all that plays in my brain is an ancient advertising jingle. For example, "You'll wonder where the yellow went when you brush your teeth with Pepsodent" will pop into my head after a conversation with some wizened local with yellowed and missing teeth. For the rest of the day, no matter what I do, this annoying verse comes back time and again to plague me. Not exactly meditation material; more like a form of torture designed to get me running and screaming from the walk.

And yet I persist.

I start a conversation with Rod or Russell, engaging in mutual moments of imagining, remembering, or speculating about the reason why something is like it is. "Why did the Romans build these roads with this kind of cobblestone? Why do you think so many people are walking the Camino this year? I wonder why …. I was thinking that …. Where do the women hang out?"

Between my aching feet and my menstruating body, my commitment to a positive attitude is being put to the test. Apparently my challenges aren't over yet.

Olveiroa can't come soon enough, and it's close to six o'clock when we finally arrive. When I stagger in to the only municipal *albergue* in the village, the *hospitalera* informs us, "Every bed is taken. There is no room here for you." I'm stunned. When I ask about other places to stay, she says, "There is only one pension in this town and it is full, too." I can sense that she is about to turn us away. I'm ready to burst into tears. Perhaps she sees the look on my face, perhaps the agony of walking is etched in my expression. Whatever the reason, she changes her mind.

And here unfolds one of the strangest experiences I've had on the Camino so far. As the *hospitalera* explains, in Spanish, that she will allow us and other late arrivals to sleep on mattresses on the floor of a separate room, an overly solicitous pilgrim decides he will help us by translating what she is saying —wait for it—into Spanish. This pilgrim insists on being the middleman in our discussion. It is too bizarre, and he ends up making the entire exchange take a whole lot longer than it need be. At the end of a very long and difficult day, my patience is thinner than a fingernail. I somehow manage to be gracious.

Because we are the first arrivals assigned to the overflow sleeping quarters, we have our pick of the mattresses. I am thankful for such small creature comforts in this uncomfortable setting. Russell is still not feeling well, and although he falls asleep first he is up a number of times in the night. His movements wake me each time.

I just want this ordeal to be over.

CHAPTER 31

I heard rain on the roof whenever I was awake last night, and it's still raining this morning when it is time to leave. Thankfully, as my period is coming to an end, my energy is returning back to normal. And after yesterday's long distance, my body still is able to move without too much difficulty.

As we huddle over our meagre breakfast, Russell asks, "What are the options for our walk today?"

Rod: "We could go twenty-one kilometres to Corcubion, or nineteen to Cée."

Russell: "Why are you lisping?"

Rod: "The guidebook says that the 'c' is pronounced as a soft 'th' sound, like at the end of the word 'teeth.'"

Russell: "Oh, so it's 'Thee by the thea.'"

Me: "Let's 'thee' what the accommodation is like in each place."

We're all turning into wise-asses. Flipping through

the guidebook, I see that if the one *albergue* in Corcubion is full, all the alternative places to stay cost more than we want to spend.

Russell: "So what are our options for tonight?"
Me: "There's less expensive places in Cée."

Rod: "Then let's stop there. Given what it's been like the last two nights, I don't want to put all my hopes on the pilgrim hostel having any room for us. Especially because we're arriving so much later than everyone else."

So Cée it is. Russell jokingly says, "This will be a cakewalk." It's only nineteen kilometres to after all.

So off we go, walking through sections of heavily forested countryside. We observe large plantations with row upon row of eucalyptus trees, a non-native species brought into Spain in the nineteenth century because of its ability to grow as much as four metres every three years. The undergrowth of eucalyptus forests is much more barren than that of indigenous oak tree forests. I read in the guidebook that the sticky sap from the eucalyptus may be harmful to birds. By contrast, the oak tree forests are rich with bird life, small shrubs, lichens, and moss. The path also wanders near large fields of blooming heather and small farms, each with its obligatory tractor by the fence line adjacent to the trail. Although much of the Santiago to Finisterre section is on paved roads, I continue to be surprised that cars travel on these skinny pieces of tarmac. Sometimes I marvel that we are still alive considering the distances we have travelled on such narrow roads, barely one lane wide, with no shoulders. Cars roar up suddenly behind us, or tear around blind corners. Even at the end of the day when we are tired, we stay alert for traffic. Yesterday I especially was thankful for the dark chocolate from the specialty shop in Santiago that kept me awake on a hard-to-keep-going day.

Our guidebook tells us that we will encounter our first views of the Atlantic Ocean before we get to Cée. I keep peering through the fog and mist that hovers above the ground, hoping to see something that looks like water. Finally the fog lifts enough for me to get my first glimpse of the ocean below. I can feel my heart racing a little faster at this sign that we are approaching the end, not just of our day, but of our long walk. Just before we enter Cée, the rain and low clouds kindly clear off to reveal the beautiful town we will stay in tonight. We are back to whitewashed walls and red ceramic tile roofs, similar to what we saw in the village of Saint Jean Pied de Port where we started this trek. It's like I'm coming full circle.

Tonight we are ensconced in a comfortable pension, affordable for us, with the biggest bathtub and the hottest water I have experienced in Spain. For a tired pilgrim body, this is the closest to bliss I could ask for. But if I did ask for more it would have to be dinner served to me by room service after Rod and I have made love. Once I have love-making on my mind, I can't stop thinking about my ever-so-scarce sex life as a pilgrim. As our walking time is drawing to a close, I'm feeling more and more physical desire. It's not just about my body's healthy response to sensual deprivation. It's also about my shift into knowing I want to stay in my relationship, that in spite of my irritations and frustrations, I've come to a deep realization that Rod is a good man at his core. He has been trustworthy since I've known him, it's been my monkey-mind that doubts when he is five minutes late coming home. I can no longer ignore all the ways that Rod is a man of his word, and a generous one at that. When he goes out to find bread for our lunches, he doesn't come back with just one loaf. Now what's not to appreciate about that?

The best man at our wedding, John, spoke about Rod's many fine qualities. At the end of his speech, John turned to me and said, "Remember, Rod is a gentle man with no malicious intentions." I can attest to that truth. He's been a devoted parent since before our children were born, and I've seen how he is willing to grow and take chances with our son on this trip. He has listened to Russell's feedback and challenges to be honest, and started to make changes in communication. I hear the word "I" much more often today that I did in Saint Jean Pied de Port where we started.

"I'm looking forward to the end of the walking."

"I'm feeling tired, I need a break."

"I love the colours of the houses along this route. They match the layers of soil in that hillside cut."

This seemingly simple shift into I-statements connects me more deeply to this man I am married to. It might take him a while to embrace challenge, but eventually he steps forward into the unknown. Maybe entering into the language of "I" is as scary to him as navigating in a strange city is to me. *Have we been guides for each other all this time?* While I float along in my dreamtime, I shift from irritation to gratitude knowing I can count on Rod to support my return to the moment.

I've been noticing that Rod is not always the serious, "just the facts" kind of guy. Over the last several days, I've enjoyed the times when he's willing to be playful, co-creating stories from images around us. Like the time in Ponferrada when our trio walked around the Castle of the Templars, making up a male version of Rapunzel— our son Russell—letting down his long hair. I love the moments when Rod shares from his imagination, giving me glimpses into the creative way he sees the world.

"This grove of trees looks like a place where faeries would gather at night."

"I wonder what stories the original owner of this broken-down hut would tell us if she was still alive."

"Look at that tree trunk; do you see the face just below the large branch?"

We may have lost sight of each other for a while, but now I feel the conviction of my decision. I want to be in this relationship, with this man. My inner "yes" to recommitment feels totally aligned. No doubts, no "what-ifs." I am grounded in this choice, prepared to speak at the right time. Rod deserves at least that much.

Yes, it has taken a heck of a lot of walking to come to this point, along with deep silence and paying attention to my meandering mind.

My decision to say "Yes" to this relationship comes with conditions. I'm still working these out. But getting to Yes feels significant. And with that Yes comes an opening of my physical desire, to share my heart and my body with my man.

I am tired of the routine of staying in *albergues,* of pulling out my *Credencial* to be stamped at the registration desk, waiting to be assigned to a bunk bed in a dormitory with twenty or forty others. I've lost interest in talking to other pilgrims. My pilgrim-self is shutting down, needing a break. I look forward to accommodations with more amenities and more privacy. One more day to walk and we will be in Finisterre. I can hardly take this in. I've been so immersed in getting to the end that I haven't really thought much about what comes next. I think something strange has happened to my brain, when I can look at a map and think, wow, I only had to walk nineteen kilometres today.

Only? When did that happen?

CHAPTER 32

MAY 17, DAY 29
CÉE TO FINISTERRE
(19 KM)

Those mixed feelings about endings I had in Santiago have surfaced even more intensely today, the last day of walking our Camino. I have fallen more in love with the simplicity and rhythm of a long walk than I ever thought possible, even with my foot cramps, aches, and pains along the way. If I could do whatever I wanted when we get to Finisterre, I would sit down to start planning our next walking journey. I am so entranced with pilgrim travel, I wonder how I will adjust when I return to the life I left behind all those weeks ago.

Thankfully we're not heading home right away. Our trio will fly to Barcelona together, then split up. Rod and I plan to explore the city while Russell participates in a Magic the Gathering Grand Prix tournament. The Barcelona Grand Prix is one of a series of international events held each year, with prize money for players who place high enough in the standings, as well as qualifying some players for the Professional Tour, a series of invite-only events with larger cash prizes and greater prestige. Once Russell connects with his gaming buddies, Rod and I will have some precious time to share our respective pilgrim journeys.

We still have the final thirteen kilometres to walk and I hear my mother's voice whisper in my ear, "Dreaming isn't going to get you there."

Well, Valentine, it's gotten me this far. And I'm not changing anything about me now.

On this final day, we are blessed with great weather. Although the guidebook warns that pilgrims seldom get a sunny day in Finisterre, my prayers to Saint Anthony have been answered. Since mid-morning, we've had clear skies and wide open vistas of the Atlantic Ocean. The city comes into sight as we make our way along the high cliff trail which parallels the ocean. Waves crash against the rocky shore, throwing up white spray in a dramatic display of nature's power. Finisterre is nestled within a curve of land, a protected harbour bordered by a long sandy beach. A safe place to land, a place for sailors to shelter from Atlantic storms. I have no words for this moment; all I want to do is leap into the air with a huge smile on my face!

The trail drops down to sea level, and we have a choice to make. Straight ahead along the boardwalk that takes us directly into the city, or take a left to meander along the beach to eventually meet up with the trail. I can't resist the indirect option. I look at Rod and Russell and they're right there with me heading toward the beach. I am drawn to the turquoise-blue water like I'm returning home. The colour reminds me of tropical oceans, although I know the water temperature will be anything but warm. The contrast of azure blue, white foaming waves, white sand beach, and blue sky overhead prompts me to pause in pure bliss. I stop to take it all in, turning in a complete circle.

"I'm arriving, I've arrived, I'm here!"

I am totally oblivious to the weight on my back, absorbed by the beauty of the shells and rocks around me. While the waves rush continuously onto the beach, I'm searching for unusual shapes mounded in the sand. The smell of salt water and sea weed are so familiar to me from beaches back home, I want to weep with recognition. Yet my greatest joy comes when I pick up an intact flat scallop shell, the symbol of pilgrims on this journey. Now I have a memento of my walk, one that I have earned. I feel connected to generations of pilgrims before me; this is an ancient tradition. Russell and Rod each proudly hold their own scallop shell finds. I pick up other shells and some ocean-polished beach stones, some of which will become offerings for the next significant places on my journey.

I start humming to myself, imagining the lyric as I do: *I'm picking up good vibrations, I'm getting excitations ....* After nearly thirty days on the trail, I am convinced there is a song for everything. Earlier this morning I hummed a chorus or two of *Here Comes the Sun*, one of the songs that I often sang after an overcast or rainy morning, which the province of Galicia delivered for at least part of each day. Finally we come to the end of the beach; we are now at the city edges. It makes sense for us to find the hotel we booked last night before we do anything else; it's still too early for lunch. We locate our home for the night on a hillside above the main commercial centre of Finisterre. The view from our bedroom window overlooks the ocean and the city below. For our final night on the trail, Rod and I have arranged for Russell to sleep in his own room. We will have couple privileges with privacy and full bath.

Four Dutch pilgrims we've met before are also staying at this hotel so we haven't completely left behind the Camino. It's always energizing to meet familiar faces, and communicate in whatever ways we can. By the time we are ready to head back downtown, it's close to Spanish lunchtime. We walk into a restaurant with its door propped open, inviting us to come in with smells of spices and seafood on the grill. The place is empty, so we check in with the rather grim-faced woman standing behind the bar. "Are you serving lunch now?"

"No."

She's obviously a woman of few words.

"When does lunchtime start here?"

"At one-thirty"

We check our watches. It's twenty-five minutes after one. So I ask, "Can we sit and wait until lunch time?"

She shrugs her shoulders as if to say, "If you must."

At one-thirty, her demeanour transforms into friendly as she walks over to our table to hand us menus.

We don't linger over the food this afternoon. Instead we press onward, on foot for our final two kilometres to Cabo Finisterre, a rocky headland where the ultimate route marker stands like a sentinel, a beacon for pilgrims who choose to finish on the coast. When I spot the marker, I run toward it, thrilled beyond belief. "Here I am! End of the Walk. End of the Earth!" The marker reads 0.00 km on the distance plaque, under the familiar yellow scallop-shell symbol on the blue background. The three of us are laughing and giggling like young children. Russell falls to his knees, hugging the stone monument, a huge grin on his face. "I made it!" Rod is quieter, happily snapping photos of us hamming it up. We take turns being the photographer and the subject.

Many snapshots later, we move on to the lighthouse, where we find the bronze statue of a pair of walking boots, another symbol for the end of the journey. Apparently the boots symbolize the practice of some pilgrims who destroy their boots to mark the end of the walk. I'm keeping my boots, thank you very much. I have more walks to take in them. The sun beams down on us and I feel truly blessed at this moment.

Russell insists we head down to the ocean, "We have to dip our toes into the Atlantic Ocean. It's another pilgrim tradition."

I grumble back, "Too bad we didn't think of this when we were beach-combing on the way into the city. It would have been a lot easier."

Russell reminds me, "We weren't officially done yet." He is somewhat of a stickler for following the rules.

Even though there are hordes of visitors unloading

from bus tours at Cabo Finisterre, Russell manages to detect a small path down to the water's edge where we find a secluded spot. I blithely follow him, swept up in a tide of happiness, immersed in a sensory experience of water meeting rocky cliffs, sun glinting off water, blue sky and puffy white clouds overhead. Rod makes a more cautious descent. I look behind and see him carefully navigating the rocks as he stops at a spot above us. He's never been comfortable on the edges of high places, and this perch above the ocean is obviously making him nervous. But, I love it here, so I find a comfortable rock to rest against for a while. I look out at the water glinting in the sunlight, drops of moisture on my skin from the wild seas below, and I consider what I have accomplished.

Russell's words echo in my head, "I made it!" I say to myself, *Me too!*

Within a few moments Rod declares, "I'm done. I don't like being in this place. I'll meet you back at the bronze boot statue." He's moving at surprising speed, much faster than when he came down. I watch him clamber up toward the lighthouse, then turn back to enjoying the view, sun on water, wind on my face, until I have my fill, waiting until I am truly ready to leave. Prior to the Camino I would have felt responsible for Rod's discomfort sitting here on the cliffs at the edge of the Atlantic Ocean. My pre-Camino response would be to start climbing back before I was ready, feeling resentful, managing what I interpreted as his unease. Perhaps this Camino journey has taught me to start saying yes to my own needs.

Russell and I leave at the same time to rejoin Rod. Russell then makes another request. "Let's climb *Monte de Facho* and stay up there until the sun drops below the horizon." He's referring to the viewpoint high above the lighthouse. "Sounds good to me," I say. Rod shrugs his shoulders and goes along with us. His silence suggests he's not too keen but still willing to participate. So off we climb until we get to the top, each of us looking for a boulder to rest against in this overlook above the ocean. I do my best to hang out amongst the rocks, morphing into my lizard-self, absorbing the heat of the sun. We don't talk; there's no need for words. It's a time of quiet reflection, as the conversations of others ebb and swirl around us, some incredibly loud and oblivious to the silent reclining pilgrims right next to where they're seated.

"Hey, buddy, give me a cigarette."

"You're always bumming smokes off me. You're such a mooch."

"Hey, did you talk to that girl last night?"

"Nah, she was too busy with her friends."

"You're such a loser."

"We need to find a different place to party tonight."

Have we blended into the landscape that well?

Minutes blend into hours, and the sun stays high in the sky. Finally, Rod hits his limit.

"Okay, I need to go now. I've had enough. I'm getting hungry, and the sun is a long way off from setting."

I'm grateful for Rod's statement. I was starting to think the same thing, but was doing my best to hang in there for Russell. Disappointment is evident in his drooping shoulders, a shadow of a frown on his face. "I really want to stay for the sunset."

I suggest, "You can stay as long as you want, and then meet us at the hotel when you're done."

He reluctantly picks up his pack, "Oh, that's okay. I'm actually hungry too."

Then I have an idea. "If it matters that much, we can arrange to come back in a taxi."

No one votes for that plan, so we say our goodbyes to Cabo Finisterre in whatever way we need to and make our way into town, following a different trail back. We manage to avoid the roadway for most of our return. Once we re-enter the city, we search for a place to have our celebration meal. We walk by a place advertising "The finest Paella." Rod says, "I don't need to look any further. Let's go in here."

Sitting in the restaurant we examine our menus, salivating as we read the meal descriptions. I had no idea there were so many different versions of paella and I want to try them all. It takes us a while to make our decisions, and during that time, a server comes by to take our drink order. It's *cerveza* all around. *"Frio, por favor!"* We clink our bottles together and Russell announces, "No more *Menu del Dia*!"

A light bulb goes off in my head. "You're right! From now on we can eat whatever we want."

Rod says, "Actually, we could have been eating anything we want every other night too. I was always so concerned about prices."

I say to myself, *So was I. It never even crossed my mind to eat anything but the cheapest menu offerings.*

It became so automatic that I stopped thinking about options. There were so many more choices on the menu that I hadn't even considered as possibilities. This seems like an important life lesson, something for me to unpack later when I get home.

When we finally receive our giant dish of paella, the three of us dive in and devour every last bit. And drink every drop of beer. It's truly a meal to remember.

The celebrating isn't over yet, at least not for Rod and me. When we return to the hotel, the two Dutch couples are playing a card game in the main floor common room. We pull up chairs to watch. Russell the gamer gets absorbed by the play. He's quick to understand what's going on and starts asking questions to clarify the rules. Rod and I are holding hands, sitting close to each other, both of us feeling the urge to retreat to our room. Finally, we stand up. "We're going up to bed, it's been a long day." Russell barely looks up; he's been included in the latest round of the card game. *How does he do that?*

flits through my mind and is gone. I'm much more interested in the game we're about to play, as Rod and I make our way up the stairs, our steps synchronized. It's all I can do to stop from running to our room, my mother's voice still guiding me to "act like a lady." Well, this lady enjoys her physical pleasures.

And here we are, finally, after all this time and all my questioning. The time for words has long since past; we rely now only on our senses. Soft light from one of the lamps is all we need to receive each other fully, eye to eye and heart to heart. And so our physical conversation begins, the one that starts with gentle touch, his hand on my thigh, my slow trailing palm up his back, caressing his face. Lips on lips, tongues searching. Lips on neck, lips on breasts, lips searching, seeking, tasting. A faint hint of salt. The heat of desire rising, neither of us rushing, letting the delicious tension build, and subside, build and subside, like waves upon the shore. Until finally we can stand it no longer and take the plunge, entering into the rhythm completely, fully, letting the motion rock us until we are completely spent.

"There's something to be said for delayed gratification," Rod chuckles into my ear.

"You've got that right."

Soft sounds of laughter from the card game downstairs waft up to our room.

I fall asleep on my side, nestled into the crook of his arm, my back against his chest. Spooning, I think it's called.

CHAPTER 33

MAY 18, DAY 30
RETURN TO SANTIAGO

The cost of our accommodation includes breakfast, so we head downstairs to the large dining room with floor-to-ceiling windows giving us views of the city and ocean below. Russell joins us there. The morning light streams in, illuminating the white table linens, reflecting the dark wooden floor. Tables are decorated with fresh flowers. Diners scattered throughout the room are already absorbed in their morning meal. The smell of freshly ground coffee is in the air. My room survey stops at a large table that displays a large basket of croissants, warm from the oven, yogurt, and fruit. This morning I do not hold back. I pick up a plate, serving myself until I arrive at the cook standing behind a griddle. He prepares an omelette according to my preferences, which include a piquant cheese and spicy Spanish chorizo sausage. My movements are languid, relaxed, and I'm surprised by how hungry I am. Then I recall my activity of the night before. I can't stop smiling. I'm sure the evidence is written all over my face and body: This woman has been well loved. Even if it's not that visible, I know that's how I feel.

We're in no big hurry, no *hospitalero* is rushing us out the door. Partway through our meal, Russell asks, "Any ideas about how we're going to get back to Santiago today?"

My suggestion: "We could take the bus. We'll have to find out where the station is."

Rod offers to get information. "Once we're done breakfast, I can check at the reception desk to find out when buses leave for Santiago. They probably have a schedule here."

Rod's inquiry results in an even better alternative. For a little more than bus fare, the hotel owner offers to drive the three of us and another couple back to Santiago in the early afternoon. It will be worth the extra cost to be dropped off at the address where we need to pick up the key to our pension. The Camino keeps providing.

I'm grateful to share the ride, swapping Camino stories along the way with an Australian couple we've never met before. While the men tell each other stories about map reading and navigation, she shyly says to me, "I had a lot of problems with my ankle, and there were days I wasn't sure I could go on. But I was so determined, there was no way I was going to quit. My husband was so worried about me, but I just kept walking."

She proudly shows me her delicate 24-carat gold scallop-shell necklace, purchased in Santiago by her husband. "He wanted to honour me with something special for making it to Santiago. I'm grateful we could finish our walk together."

In return, I let her know, "I had a lot of problems with my feet, and I felt the same as you. I didn't even let myself think about stopping. I just kept walking." We have a moment of shared understanding, surprised at ourselves, bonded by our tenacity and how we've reached deep inside of ourselves to have this moment.

We are truly done walking. I'm finding myself somewhat disoriented to be travelling at such high speed in a motorized vehicle. A journey that took us four days on foot is over in a few hours. How amazing is that?

At times I sit silently and gaze through the window, observing the landscape flying by, my brain clicking over as fast as the speeding car I'm riding in. I seem to have arrived at a place of acceptance about so many things. Walking long distances in rainy weather. Silly songs running through my head. Foot cramps. Predictable food choices. Shared sleeping accommodations. The repetitiveness of each day.

And finally, accepting the differences in how my partner and I perceive the world. I see with new eyes that Rod is a scientist, rooted in his logical-rational mind. While he has an intuitive side and great insights, the world of facts and linear reality dominates his inner landscape. Unlike me. It's not like one of us is right and the other is wrong. For thirty days, I have been learning to listen differently and to be open to his way of being in the world without being defensive—not always successfully.

Something about my relationship with myself has also shifted. I have persisted through all the mind-chatter, difficult memories, and unpleasant encounters. I can honestly say out loud now, "I like who I am."

It seems to me that practising gratitude and appreciation on this walk allowed me to reconnect with the qualities I was first attracted to in Rod. I've been able to receive his innate goodness once again, in a way I haven't been open to since early in our marriage.

*　*　*

We are dropped off at the café where some of our possessions await us. The owners greet us like old friends, enthusiastically retrieving the box of excess walking gear we had left with them while we went on to Finisterre. This couple also owns the pension across the street, our lodging when we first arrived in Santiago. We'll stay here again tonight, so we pay for the room and get the key. As Rod reaches for his wallet, he suddenly remembers he's left his passport on the seat of the van. We all have a brief moment of panic that calms when the male owner heads to the phone to call the driver on his cell phone. These two men know each other and it's a quick and easy explanation. In less than twenty minutes, Rod's passport has been returned to him. More Camino magic.

Tonight we stay in Santiago, sharing a room with Russell for one last time. Tomorrow we fly to Barcelona. Russell is hoping for great results at the Magic Grand Prix. Rod wants to catch up on his sleep. I'm dreaming of buying fancy shoes.

I'd like to think we will have all our wishes granted.

CHAPTER 34

MAY 19,
BARCELONA

The trip from Santiago to Barcelona happens in a blur. Now, after a one and three-quarter hour flight, here I am, settling into a spacious suite near Las Ramblas, the long pedestrian mall attractive to both tourists and locals. That stuck-between-two-worlds sensation returns. My earth-based self feels restless, as if it's still making its way here on foot. The rest of me is present in Barcelona, ready to explore. Russell is anxious to meet up with other Magic the Gathering competitors assembling in this city, and he urges us out the door. We accompany him to one of the gaming stores specializing in Magic trading cards, located near where we're staying. He sees familiar faces, immediately entering into conversations about the upcoming tournament. Once he's confirmed that he has a place to stay, we discreetly say our farewells. It's a bittersweet parting for me; I feel like mamma bear letting her cub leave the safety of the den. Saying goodbye to my children doesn't get any easier. At the same time, I feel a delicious sense of freedom, now that Rod and I are on our own.

We head off to explore Las Ramblas, drawn to the area nearest the ocean. We hold hands and saunter, eyeing the wall-to-wall market stalls occupying the centre of the street. We don't say much at this point; rather we're quietly enjoying each other's presence, knowing we don't have to rush. I reflect on the themes of gratitude and noticing beauty, how practising both supported me to complete my pilgrimage. There is much I want to say, yet in this moment I am distracted by music blaring from restaurant patios as we merge into hordes of people wandering as we are. I'm curious, open to everything around me, yet still mindful of the fact that I'm here with Rod. I marvel that we continue to enjoy each other's company, so unlike what I experienced with my parents. My surroundings feel surreal when I consider where I've come from, that small town in northern Alberta where I could only dream of lands far away.

As evening sets in we enter a restaurant advertising an extensive seafood menu. The hostess seats us on the wooden deck, at a table protected by a large umbrella. After our drinks arrive, I begin to talk about my experience of our journey. I tell Rod, "I started out feeling resentful and impatient at the beginning of the walk, but that got really tiresome. So I decided to focus on what was working well as a way to change my thinking. I had so much more energy when I started doing that."

He reflects back, "I started to notice those changes in you after the first week. Probably one of my biggest challenges was giving up control, my belief that I had to be the one who was responsible for the group. I started to realize that the three of us needed to be involved in decision-making, that it wasn't helpful when I tried to be the one taking charge. Russell was particularly insistent about having his say, and he is a great map reader and navigator."

"Well, he is your son after all. And I also like how we started to listen to each other more. I began to pay attention to everyone's needs, rather than push my own agenda. I had to let go of believing that the whole world revolves around me."

Rod offers his perspective: "We've all learned to be more accepting of each other on this long walk. We wouldn't have made it this far without kindness."

"I couldn't agree more."

Once our meals are in front of us, I feel brave enough to keep opening up: "When I focused on paying attention to the times I was grateful for your presence, I found a new perspective on our relationship."

I warn him, "Brace yourself, I'm going to keep telling you what I appreciate about you on a daily basis. I'm not waiting another twenty-five years."

He smiles back at me. "I think I can handle that."

"There's one more thing I'd like you to know. I also intend to use my words to let you know when I feel hurt or dismissed. I might say something like 'Ouch' or 'That doesn't feel good.' I'd like you to be as open with me."

"That's not going to be easy," he reveals.

"Since when did we back off when things weren't easy?"

We laugh together at that and start the long walk back to our apartment.

These few days in Barcelona are a time for us to transition from pilgrims back to city folk. It seems fitting to visit a cathedral or two while we're here. First on my list is La Sagrada Familia, a huge Roman Catholic basilica which Antoni Gaudi worked on from 1883 until he died in 1926. Almost ninety years later, this building is still under construction. His designs were inspired by close observation of nature and I'm curious to see how Gaudi's vision translates into physical form. When I arrive in front of the basilica, I see tall spires with fanciful forms piercing the sky. Scaffolds, netting, and ladders adorn the exterior. The interior is in state of disarray; pallets and building materials on the hallway floors limit the space available for visitors. Tours are offered at prices neither Rod nor I are willing to pay. Noise created by workers above us is loud enough to make us cover our ears. I signal to Rod that I would like to leave, and he nods in agreement. The sound of a jackhammer jangles our senses as we exit against the crush of people entering the building. With a glance over my shoulder at the Gaudi masterpiece, I declare, "That was more than I can handle. I think it would be more enjoyable if I visited parks rather than checking out more buildings."

Rod gets out his tourist map, and we select Parc Tibidabo as our destination for tomorrow. I read the description aloud: "located on a mountain overlooking the city." Anything that gets me up high and into nature makes me happy. Rod is particularly interested in the funicular railway, a cable tramway system that transports visitors up the mountain to the park. Still preferring to be on foot, we walk several kilometres to the base of the hillside where we buy tickets and board the funicular. When we arrive at the Parc, the first thing we do is check out the view, orienting ourselves from this vantage point.

Adjacent to the viewpoint is the Expiatory Church of the Sacred Heart of Jesus. *Yet another church?* My curiosity draws me in, Rod close behind. A priest greets us as we enter informing us that within this church is a small chapel. His presence is open and welcoming; I feel safe here. The pamphlet he hands to me describes that there has been a constant human meditative presence in the chapel since 1966. After walking around the perimeter of the cathedral, examining the religious icons and images in the stained glass windows, Rod and I slip into the chapel and take a seat. Those around us are deep in contemplative silence. Here is the peace I was seeking at La Sagrada Familia. I concentrate on my breath, joining with others on this silent journey. Without knowing I have another declaration to make to Rod, the words I need to say arrive like a drink of water after a long walk in the hot sun.

This is the essence of what I shared with Rod afterward, sitting on a bench, apart from other visitors, overlooking Barcelona:

"You may not have understood that I was considering the possibility of leaving you when we first started this journey. I want you to know that I am fully committed to staying in this relationship. What that means is I will continue to be appreciative of who you are, to notice your goodness, to be respectful, and to acknowledge my needs as well as yours. I will stay in this relationship as long as we both have a mutual commitment to treating each other with respect."

I make these statements fully prepared for whatever response comes back. I truly don't know how Rod will respond. Maybe I've said too much, pushed him too far. However without respect, we are never going to create the kind of relationship I want to be in. I am ready to let go of my resentments and shift old habit patterns. I intend to pay attention to the small details that bring joy into my life. This is my starting point, post-Camino.

Rod listens attentively but doesn't respond right away. He finally says, "I knew something was going on with you, but I didn't want to ask. I think I was afraid to hear your answer. I can't imagine ending this relationship with you. I'm in, and I want to make changes too. I like the idea of starting with respect." His eyes shift around rather than hold eye contact, his fingers dance a pattern on his knee. It will take practice before we both feel comfortable with such moments of vulnerable sharing.

We still have work to do but we know where to start. And so we begin a new journey together. Valentine is looking on. I can sense her unguarded delight, see her smile, hands clasped in a prayer.

I REMEMBER

There was a time when my mother could remember,
not that long ago, or so it seems.
Was it yesterday?
Twenty years ago?
Or a second?
Sitting still in her room while in her mind the sun warms her face
with the wind blowing off the lake
setting the gulls to wheeling in the sky,
a soft smile displaying her delight.

I remember my mother's sadness, her hard places, her anger.
So much of my child-time filled with her jagged edges
leaving me with a longing and a hunger that couldn't be fed.
That was a time I wanted to forget.
So I disappeared into a fragmented world,
a mix of imaginings and memories.
Stained glass
broken and put together
by a three-year old.

I don't recall my mom ever telling me
she loved me.
But when she could no longer remember,
her eyes were full of love
even when there was no recognition.
"Are you the nurse?" she would ask.
"No," I'd reply. "I'm your youngest daughter."
But my response had already vanished into her not-comprehending
mind.

So I would sit with her, my mom and I
holding hands
in silence.

EPILOGUE

HORNBY ISLAND

It's June and we want to celebrate Russell's birthday as a family. We're looking to create an adventure we can all enjoy together. Even though Russell wants to hike, he knows that Emma isn't a big fan of covering long distances on foot. "What about sea kayaking?" I throw out as an idea. Emma says, "Yes! Could we sea kayak somewhere on Hornby Island?" Russell has never been in a sea kayak before, so he's a bit hesitant at first. Thankfully, he's also game for something new. "Sure, why not?"

I go into planning mode, following the train of this energy. There's nothing I love more than finding ways for all four of us to do things together. "We could rent kayaks on Hornby and spend a day poking along the shoreline. I've heard about some great places for paddling there." Rod speaks up, "It will be our treat, we'll cover all the costs." And I add, mother instincts always alive, "I'll bring all the lunch and snack supplies. You and Emma just need to show up." Both kids speak at the same time, "Sounds good to me."

And that's what we create together, a sunny June day of paddling on Hornby Island, following the shoreline and exploring small bays and inlets, following whatever impulses we have for looking at ocean wonders. We marvel at where we live now. Coastal rather than prairie environment. Sea kayaking rather than river canoeing. Loving the fact that we can easily put together our family adventure on this day.

When it's time to stop for lunch, we find a protected pebble beach where we pull in to shore and draw up our kayaks so they won't float away with the incoming tide. After our feast, Emma and Russell wander off together, talking and laughing as they turn over rocks, poke sticks into tide pools, and share silly stories. Rod and I lie back in the sun, happy to stretch out our bodies after sitting in the kayak for a couple of hours. I reach for his hand and give it a squeeze.

"We did good work," I say to him.

"We sure did," he replies.

Then he asks, "Did you ever think we'd turn out like this?"

"Honestly? I never could have imagined how good our lives would be. I still can't believe that we live on Vancouver Island, in such a beautiful place. I'm amazed that our children ended up leaving Calgary to live near us. Whatever I had to go through has been so worth it. I love being here, right now with you, and with Russell and Emma."

We look up at the clouds, relaxing even further into the heat of the sun. I shift closer to Rod, our shoulders touching, enjoying that simple physical contact. The tangy, salty smell of the sea is in my nostrils, a sharp reminder that I am here beside the ocean. On a beautiful island, near our home, with the person I love and the children we have nurtured together. No words are needed, this is perfection.

I turn to Rod, making eye contact. In my mind, I'm saying *I love you* and I see his love reflected back to me.

When we first moved to Vancouver Island all I could think about was endings. I understand now it was all about beginnings.

Marie Maccagno
adventures in writing

Have you had words swirling around your head and weighing heavy on your heart for many years but never dared to put pen to paper because of a nagging inner critic holding you back? Are you at the point in your life where you are ready to invest in your self-development and say YES to YOU for a change?

Marie Maccagno leads adventures in writing through

☐ One-on-One Guidance
☐ On-going Writing Circles
☐ Retreats for Renewal and Transformation
☐ Writing Mastermind, a deep dive into loving your words

For more information contact Marie today
www.mariemaccagno.com

* * *

NOTE TO THE READER: Please visit this link to view photos from Marie's Camino walk:
www.mariemaccagno.com/the-chocolate-pilgrim-photos

Made in the USA
Columbia, SC
16 October 2017